ISAIAH
FOR YOU

TIM CHESTER
ISAIAH
FOR YOU

thegoodbook
COMPANY

Isaiah For You
© Tim Chester, 2021
Reprinted 2023

thegoodbook
COMPANY

Published by:
The Good Book Company

thegoodbook.com | thegoodbook.co.uk
thegoodbook.com.au | thegoodbook.co.nz | thegoodbook.co.in

ISBN: 9781784985585

Cover design by Ben Woodcraft | Printed in India

CONTENTS

SERIES PREFACE

Each volume of the *God's Word For You* series takes you to the heart of a book of the Bible, and applies its truths to your heart.

The central aim of each title is to be:

- Bible centred
- Christ glorifying
- Relevantly applied
- Easily readable

You can use *Isaiah For You:*

To read. You can simply read from cover to cover, as a book that explains and explores the themes, encouragements and challenges of this part of Scripture.

To feed. You can work through this book as part of your own personal regular devotions, or use it alongside a sermon or Bible-study series at your church. Each chapter is divided into two (or occasionally three) shorter sections, with questions for reflection at the end of each.

To lead. You can use this as a resource to help you teach God's word to others, both in small-group and whole-church settings. You'll find tricky verses or concepts explained using ordinary language, and helpful themes and illustrations along with suggested applications.

These books are not commentaries. They assume no understanding of the original Bible languages, nor a high level of biblical knowledge. Verse references are marked in **bold** so that you can refer to them easily. Any words that are used rarely or differently in everyday language outside the church are marked in grey when they first appear, and are explained in a glossary toward the back. There, you'll also find details of resources you can use alongside this one, in both personal and church life.

Our prayer is that as you read, you'll be struck not by the contents of this book, but by the book it's helping you open up; and that you'll praise not the author of this book, but the One he is pointing you to.

Carl Laferton, Series Editor

Bible translations used:

- NIV: New International Version, 2011 edition. (This is the version being quoted unless otherwise stated.)

- NLT: New Living Translation.

- ESV: English Standard Version.

INTRODUCTION TO ISAIAH

"You who bring good news to Zion,
    go up on a high mountain.
You who bring good news to Jerusalem,
    lift up your voice with a shout,
lift it up, do not be afraid;
    say to the towns of Judah,
    'Here is your God!'" (Isaiah 40:9)

A book of good news

Isaiah can seem somewhat intimidating. For one thing, it's a big book covering an extended timescale. Sometimes we're immersed in the politics of Isaiah's day; sometimes he's responding to events a hundred or so years in his future. It's full of unfamiliar names and places, all set in a very different culture. You may be familiar with Isaiah's vision of God's holiness in chapter 6 or his description of the cross in chapter 53. But large sections may feel like alien territory.

But the book of Isaiah is full of good news and, as 40:9 highlights, it's news worth shouting about. All the time it is pointing forward to Jesus. As a result, perhaps more than any other book in the Old Testament, Isaiah forms a kind of bridge between the Old Testament and the New Testament.

We need this book for at least seven reasons:

1. *Isaiah enlarges our view of God.* Isaiah gives us a rich vision of an eternal God of overwhelming holiness, with a passion for his glory, who shapes the course of history, fights for justice, comes to rescue his people and dwells among the lowly.

2. *Isaiah enriches our love for Christ.* Many of our favourite Christmas and Easter readings come from Isaiah because Isaiah presents a vivid portrait of Jesus as the Spirit-empowered

Messiah* who reigns in justice and the faithful Servant who saves through suffering.

3. *Isaiah sharpens our understanding of salvation.* Isaiah provides a clear picture of the saving work of Christ as an act of liberation modelled on the **exodus** from Egypt and as an act of substitution through which Christ pays the penalty of our sin.

4. *Isaiah illuminates our Bible reading.* By seeing the exodus from Egypt as a blueprint for the ultimate deliverance of God's people, Isaiah massively shaped the New Testament understanding of Christ and thereby helps us read the Old Testament story as our story.

5. *Isaiah comforts our fears and sorrows.* Isaiah brought comfort to people facing major threats and big disappointments, and so points us to the rest and peace that come from entrusting ourselves to God.

6. *Isaiah excites our vision for the church.* Isaiah gives a delightful vision of the church as a community of justice, clothed in divine splendour, which brings light to the world and draws the nations to the ways of the Lord.

7. *Isaiah fuels our commitment to mission.* He invites us to lift our eyes from our parochial concerns to see God gathering people from the four corners of the world through the global mission of the church.

An orientation to the life and work of Isaiah

Isaiah 1:1 sets the prophet's **ministry** in its historical context: "The vision concerning Judah and Jerusalem that Isaiah son of Amoz saw during the reigns of Uzziah, Jotham, Ahaz and Hezekiah, kings of **Judah**." This means Isaiah ministered about 800 years before Christ.

---

* Words in **grey** are defined in the Glossary (page 213).

Here are some key dates and events for understanding his life and message.

■ *739 BC: King Uzziah dies.* Isaiah 6 describes Isaiah's vision of God in the temple and his commission to "go and tell [the] people" (6:9). This is often called Isaiah's call, but its position in the book suggests his ministry may have begun before this event. The vision took place "in the year that King Uzziah died", which was 739 BC. Uzziah's reign had been long and prosperous (he reigned 791-739). But now Tiglath-Pileser III, the king of Assyria, was threatening Judah. Assyria was to the north of Judah, and at this point in time it was emerging as the regional superpower.

■ *734 BC: Israel and Aram threaten Judah.* Isaiah ministered at a time when the twelve tribes of Israel had split into two nations: the ten northern tribes, who were known as Israel or Ephraim, and the two southern tribes, who were known as Judah (where Isaiah was active). Isaiah 7 describes the alliance between King Pekah of Israel and King Rezin of Aram against King Ahaz of Judah. Isaiah exhorts Ahaz (who co-reigned or reigned 735-715) to trust in God, but instead Ahaz looks to Assyria.

■ *701 BC: Sennacherib besieges Jerusalem.* Isaiah 36 – 39 describes the attack on Jerusalem by Sennacherib, the king of the Assyrian Empire. By then the king of Judah was Hezekiah, who reigned 729-686 (including a period when he reigned alongside his father). King Hezekiah turns to God in prayer, and Jerusalem is dramatically delivered.

■ *587 BC: Exile into Babylon.* In time the Assyrian Empire gave way to the Babylonian Empire, also located to the north of Judah (in modern-day Iraq). The Babylonians would defeat Judah and destroy Jerusalem in 587 BC, leading many of the people away into exile (including Ezekiel and Daniel). Isaiah predicts this exile and the Babylonian captivity of Judah in 587 BC. In chapters 40 – 66 Isaiah addresses these exiles—speaking into a situation two centuries after his day. But these chapters also look beyond this judgment to offer the hope of a new exodus through which God will gather his exiled people home to a restored land.

You may find it helpful to keep the following outline in mind so that you can set the details of what you're reading in the big picture of Isaiah's overall message. I've also highlighted some of the names of God that come to the fore in each section.

Chapters	Initial Audience and Historical Context	Threat or Empire	Central Message
1 – 6	The "overture"— a medley of key themes.		The Holy King judges fruitless Jerusalem, but will renew her.
7 – 12	Isaiah invites King Ahaz to trust God rather than form an alliance with Assyria.	Aram & Israel	The LORD Almighty promises a new King.
13 – 27	Isaiah addresses the nations.		The LORD Almighty will rule the nations through his King.
28 – 39	Isaiah invites King Hezekiah to trust God rather than form an alliance with Egypt.	Assyria	Human help is useless, but the Holy One of Israel gives rest.
40 – 55	Isaiah looks ahead to the exile in Babylon.	Babylon	I AM will redeem his people in a new exodus through the sufferings of the Servant.
56 – 66	Isaiah looks ahead to the return from exile.	Persia	The Warrior-God will gather his people from all nations through the mission of his servants.

Reading the book of Isaiah

In each chapter of this book I've focused on one passage (indicated below the title) within the chapters of Isaiah under consideration. At the same time, although I've not provided detailed comments on every verse, I have tried to show how this passage is representative. In this way we will see the overall message of Isaiah. I hope, too, it might provide some pointers to those wanting to preach through Isaiah or study it in a small group.

For those who want to read through the whole of Isaiah, I've also provided a "reader's guide" in each chapter of this book. This offers a brief orientation to each chapter of Isaiah, along with some pointers to the way Isaiah's prophecy is fulfilled in Christ and his people.

Authors sometimes use an introduction to suggest how readers ought to read the book they have written. What advice would Isaiah give us as we approach his book? In 33:5-6 he says:

"The LORD ... will be the sure foundation for your times,
a rich store of salvation and wisdom and knowledge;
the fear of the LORD is the key to this treasure."

Towards the end of the book God himself says:

"These are the ones I look on with favour:
those who are humble and contrite in spirit,
and who tremble at my word." (66:2)

As with any book of the Bible, the real key to unlocking the treasures in the book of Isaiah is to fear the LORD and tremble at his word. We're not to come expecting to judge the value of what we read. Instead, we're to come with a humble and contrite spirit, expecting to be judged by the word. But we can also expect that through his word God will give us a foundation for our times, a rich store of wisdom and an experience of his favour.

1. GOD REVEALS HIS HOLINESS

FOCUS: ISAIAH 6

The American pastor A.W. Tozer famously said, "What comes into our minds when we think about God is the most important thing about us." He went on:

> "For this reason the gravest question before the Church is always God Himself, and the most portentous fact about any man is not what he at a given time may say or do, but what he in his deep heart conceives God to be like. We tend by a secret law of the soul to move toward our mental image of God."
>
> (*The Knowledge of the Holy*, p 1)

One danger is to think of God simply as a bigger or better version of ourselves. We assume God is like us, but with more power or greater moral consistency. We think of ourselves first and then make God in our likeness. That's the wrong way round. We only discover the truth about ourselves as we truly see God. Isaiah 6 describes a vision of God that became the defining perspective of Isaiah's life and ministry.

Reader's guide

Isaiah 1

*Isaiah 1 – 5 previews some of the key themes in the rest of the book, so it is not easy to link these speeches or **oracles** to specific historical events. In chapter 1 Isaiah condemns God's people for their rebellion against God and their injustice towards one another (1:2-17, 21-31).*

But judgment can be averted if the people repent (1:18-20)—an offer that was not taken up. The "faithful city has become a prostitute" (1:21), but "afterwards you will be called the City of Righteousness, the Faithful City" (1:26).

Isaiah 2

Isaiah contrasts the glorious long-term future of Jerusalem (2:1-5) with the present reality of her sin and impending judgment (2:6-22). Isaiah's vision of a city on hill attracting the nations is picked up again in Isaiah 60 and fulfilled in the church (Matthew 5:14). First God's people must be humbled. The "refrain" of this section is: "The eyes of the arrogant will be humbled and human pride brought low; the LORD alone will be exalted in that day" (2:11; see also 2:17 and 5:15-16).

Isaiah 3 - 4

God is going to take his people to court, and the verdict will be condemnation (3:13-15). Their leadership will fail (3:1-12), and their finery will be lost (3:16 – 4:1). But God also promises to restore "the Branch of the LORD" (4:2). Elsewhere this describes God's promised King (Jeremiah 23:5), but here it appears to refer to God's people. God will wash away their guilt (4:3-4) and protect them as he did in the wilderness after the exodus (4:5-6)—promises ultimately fulfilled when Jesus cleanses us from guilt and leads us home to God.

Isaiah 5

Isaiah sings a love song in which God's people are a vineyard that God has tended. But God is going to destroy his vineyard because it produces only bad fruit (5:1-7). (This image is graciously reversed in 27:2-6.) Isaiah then proclaims six woes against his people (5:8-25). God is going to whistle to the nations (as we might whistle for a dog to come), and they will come to judge God's people (5:26-30).

Isaiah 6

In chapter 6 this message becomes personal as Isaiah himself sees a vision of God's power and holiness. This vision defines his ministry (he often refers to God as "the Holy One of Israel"). Isaiah volunteers to go *as God's messenger, but his ministry will only harden people in their rebellion against God.*

The LORD is King

Chapter 6 begins by locating this vision at a particular moment in history towards the beginning of Isaiah's career (fully outlined in 1:1). Isaiah **6:1*** begins, "In the year that King Uzziah died". King Uzziah had reigned for 52 years (having been crowned when he was only 16 years old). "He sought God during the days of Zechariah, who instructed him in the fear of God. As long as he sought the LORD, God gave him success" (2 Chronicles 26:5). His was something of a golden age of peace and prosperity (2 Chronicles 26:1-15).

But now the winds of change were blowing. The old king had died, and the Assyrian Empire was like a dark cloud on the horizon. In this time of uncertainty and insecurity, what Isaiah sees is the true King.

God is first introduced as "the Lord". This is not God's **covenant** name, "Yahweh" (depicted in our English Bibles with capital letters). This word means "Lord", "sovereign" or "master". It describes God's role rather than his identity. God is the Sovereign who rules the earth. Isaiah calls him "the King" in **6:5**. **Verse 1** continues, "I saw the Lord, high and exalted, seated on a throne". It's a royal description. Even today we talk about "Your Royal Highness" and monarchs "ascend" to the throne. A king or queen sits on a raised platform so that even when they are seated, they're higher than anyone else. Here in Isaiah's vision the Lord is physically above everyone else to show the supremacy of his power.

When Queen Elizabeth II was crowned in 1953, she wore the Robe of State, six yards of hand-woven silk velvet lined with ermine. It was so heavy that it required seven ladies-in-waiting to carry it. Think how impractical that is—it's an item of clothing that you can't walk in! But the point was to highlight her majesty and power. Isaiah sees God

---

* All verse references from the main passage in focus in each chapter are in **bold**.

wearing a royal robe. But it's not six yards long. Isaiah says, "The train of his robe filled the **temple**". It's wrapping round and round to fill the entire space. It's all designed to emphasise the supreme majesty and ultimate power of God.

Uzziah has gone; Assyria is coming. But God remains on the throne. We, too, live in times of change. Indeed, the rate of change at times feels dizzying. For many of us, the future feels full of foreboding. The church in the West is in decline and our values are marginalised. But God is still the Lord on the throne—just as he was in the year that King Uzziah died.

The LORD is holy

Isaiah **6:2** says, "Above him were seraphim, each with six wings: with two wings they covered their faces, with two they covered their feet, and with two they were flying." Seraphim are angelic beings, made by God to attend him in his heavenly court. What Isaiah is interested in is their anatomy. They have six wings: two for moving around and four for covering their eyes and feet in God's presence. These are beings which have never sinned. You might think that puts them on a moral par with God. But not sinning is just the negative. What God also possesses are the positive attributes of holiness and purity. And he possesses them with such intensity that the seraphim, even though they have never sinned, must expend two-thirds of their energy simply on protecting themselves from God's holiness.

The reality of God's holiness that Isaiah *sees* in the seraphim's wings is matched by what he hears from their lips: "Holy, holy, holy is the LORD Almighty" (**6:3**). In English, if we want to emphasise a word, we can underline it or put it in bold font. The Hebrew language achieves the same effect by repeating the word. So Genesis 14:10 speaks of "the tar pits". It's literally "the pit-pit of tar". In other words, this is the most pit-like pit of tar. Or 2 Kings 25:15 talks about bowls made of "gold-gold"—the goldest of gold or, as the NIV translates it, "pure gold". Jesus does the same thing. When he wants to emphasise something, he introduces it with the words "Truly, truly". The NIV translates it as "I tell you the truth". It's literally "Amen, amen". This is the truest truth. Here in Isaiah 6 we hear the song of heaven. And what they sing is not just that God is holy-holy. God is not just the holiest of holy beings. Uniquely in the Bible, we get a *tripling* of intensity. They sing that God is the holiest of holiest of holy beings.

> This is Mount Sinai all over again, and Isaiah is bang in the middle of it.

So Isaiah *sees* the holiness of God highlighted by the three pairs of wings on the seraphim, and he *hears* the holiness of God highlighted by their three-fold cry. Then, to complete the full sensory experience, he *feels* the holiness of God as the doorposts shake, and he smells the holiness of God as smoke fills the temple (**6:4**).

After God delivered his people from slavery in Egypt, he met with them at Mount Sinai. "Mount Sinai was covered with smoke, because the LORD descended on it in fire. The smoke billowed up from it like smoke from a furnace, and the whole mountain trembled violently," says Exodus 19:18. The cloud was there to shield the people from the sight of God's glory. Even the priests could not step onto the mountain, otherwise "the LORD [would] break out against them" (Exodus 19:22). The **tabernacle** and, later, the temple were built in part as permanent representations of this experience. The altar of incense, which stood before the curtain that separated off the **Holy of Holies**, was basically a kind of smoke machine, creating a permanent cloud of smoke to replicate the event of Mount Sinai.

And now Isaiah stands in the middle of all this noise and smoke. This is Mount Sinai all over again, and he's bang in the middle of it. And in his mind must surely have been the words, "The LORD will break out against them".

Not only that, but a few months before someone else had stood where Isaiah now stands. King Uzziah had for the most part been a good king, but his reign had ended in tragedy. "After Uzziah became powerful," we're told in 2 Chronicles 26:16, "his pride led to his downfall". He went into the temple to offer incense on the altar of incense. When a group of "courageous priests" confronted him, Uzziah started "raging" against them. But, as he did so, the Lord afflicted him with leprosy. He had to be led from the temple and spent the few remaining months of his life in disgraced isolation (2 Chronicles 26:16-21).

So what does Isaiah think when he finds himself in the temple? Uzziah's judgment is still hot news. The last time someone stood where Isaiah is standing, they were struck down by God.

God's holiness is not so much an attribute of God as the perfection and intensity of all his other attributes. God's holiness is the perfection of his love, power, purity, wisdom, and justice. He is perfect love and purest purity. He has the wisest strength and the strongest wisdom. The Bible describes God as a consuming fire. Think of the white-hot heat of a bonfire. It's compelling. You can't take your eyes off it, and yet you feel its danger. Our God is a consuming fire, burning with the intensity of his holiness like the burning centre of a star. Anything tainted by sin is consumed in the presence of his powerful purity and perfect love.

Questions for reflection

1. Can you identify with Isaiah's sense of woe before the holy God? How does this passage help you have a greater sense of God's holiness?

2. When Isaiah saw this vision, his nation was full of fear for the future. When you feel afraid or uncertain, how does it help to remember God's sovereign power?

3. As you yourself get to know God better, what will you do or say in response to who he is?

PART TWO

The holiness of God is a threat to sinful people, and Isaiah finds himself immersed in a full-on sensory experience of God's holiness. We're told in **6:1** that the train of God's robe *fills* the temple. Isaiah is standing in the temple, and all around him is God's robe. It's in front of him, behind him, and on either side. If someone steps into your personal space, you sidle away; you retreat. But there's nowhere for Isaiah to go. God's holiness surrounds him.

The Hebrew word for "glory" comes from the word "weight". In English we talk about "weighty ideas" or a "heavy blow". So for Isaiah it feels as if God's glory and holiness are pressing in on him from every side and through every sense. He feels like he's being crushed by the weight of divine glory. He sees it, hears it, feels it, smells it. It's the moral version of being squeezed and squeezed with nowhere to run, no place to hide, no power to resist.

So Isaiah cries out, "Woe to me! I am ruined!" (**6:5**). Back in 3:11 Isaiah had said, "Woe to the wicked! Disaster is upon them! They will be paid back for what their hands have done." But now, standing before the holiness of God, Isaiah himself cries, "Woe to *me!*" He recognises that he is one of the wicked and disaster is upon *him*. Similarly, in chapter 5 Isaiah declared woe on other people six times:

1. "Woe to you who add house to house" (5:8-10).

2. "Woe to those who rise early ... to run after their drinks" (5:11-17).

3. "Woe to those who draw sin along with cords of deceit" (5:18-19).

4. "Woe to those who call evil good and good evil" (5:20).

5. "Woe to those who are wise in their own eyes" (5:21).

6. "Woe to those who are heroes at drinking wine" (5:22-30).

But the seventh woe Isaiah declares against *himself*. "Woe to you" becomes "Woe to me".

I wonder if you've made that movement yet. You can readily see the faults of other people. Maybe you feel quite good in comparison. But have you stood before the holiness of God and cried, "Woe to *me*"?

The phrase "I am ruined" (**6:5**) is literally "I'm destroyed" or even "I'm disintegrating". It's as if the very molecules of Isaiah's body are dissolving or about to crumble to the ground. God's holiness presses in on Isaiah, and he feels crushed. Isaiah uses the same word in 15:1 to describe the destruction of a city. Think of a city destroyed by war, full of bombed-out buildings and piles of rubble. That's what Isaiah's soul feels like when faced with the reality of God. A friend once said of someone we both knew, "If he realised the impact of his actions on other people, it would crush him". In reality that's true of us all. It's only before God that we attain true self-knowledge—and it's devastating.

Isaiah was a good man, one of the best. He did many good things. But sin has infected the very fibre of our beings. Our problem is not so much that we do sinful acts but that we *are* sinners. You can't remedy sin just by trying harder or turning over a new leaf. That's like treating gangrene by putting on make-up. If you think you're basically ok, you've not grasped the terrifying holiness and majesty of God. You will only get a true view of yourself when you get a true view of God.

> You only get a true view of yourself when you get a true view of God.

It gets worse. You may recognise that some parts of your life have been unclean, but then you comfort yourself with the thought that at least you serve God in other ways. "This week," you might say to yourself, "I've not thrown a punch, looked at porn, shouted in anger, cheated with my expenses—I've not done that badly." But look at what Isaiah says: "I am a man of unclean lips, and I live among a people of unclean *lips*" (**6:5**). Remember, Isaiah was a prophet. He was gifted by God and called by God to speak God's word with his lips. The main way he served God was *with his lips*. Yet when he sees God's holiness, he recognises that even his service of God is tainted by sin.

Isaiah 64:6 says, "All of us have become like one who is unclean"—in other words, what Isaiah experienced as he stood before God's holiness is true of everyone—"and all our righteous acts are like filthy rags".

Do you feel that? Maybe you think of all the ways you serve God, and, when you compare yourself to other people, you think, "Yes, I'm a pretty good Christian." Imagine Isaiah stumbling from this vision to the house of a friend and repeating his words, "I am a man of unclean lips." We might well imagine the friend saying, "But you're the greatest preacher of your generation!" It's not going to console Isaiah. When you stop comparing yourself with other people and start comparing yourself with God, you look at even your good works and say, "Woe is me." I've been a Christian for over 40 years, and I sometimes wonder if I've ever done a good act. My good deeds may look good from the outside, but underneath every single one is stained with pride, selfishness or self-reliance. What makes Isaiah cry out, "Woe to me", "I am ruined" and "I am unclean" is this: "my eyes have seen the King, the LORD Almighty" (**6:5**). If you have a big view of yourself, it's because you have a small view of God.

In Isaiah's vision God's glory fills the temple (**6:1**). But what the seraphim sing is this: "The *whole earth* is full of his glory" (**6:3**). The temple does not contain the threat posed by God's holiness in the way that, for example, the concrete which now encases the Chernobyl nuclear reactor contains its threat. What Isaiah sees is a visual representation of the God before whom we must all one day stand. Try to imagine that. I don't know exactly what it will be like, but one day the holiness of God will press in on our consciousness, and it will feel like we're disintegrating. Our future is *ruin*.

The LORD is gracious

But it need not be; for the third thing we see in Isaiah's vision is that the Lord is gracious:

"Then one of the seraphim flew to me with a live coal in his hand, which he had taken with tongs from the altar. With it he

touched my mouth and said, 'See, this has touched your lips;
your guilt is taken away and your sin **atoned** for.'" (**6:6-7**)

Our problem is the utter incompatibility of God's holiness and our
guilt. Moreover, God cannot stop being holy, and we cannot stop being guilty. Even if we could, there's a backlog of unaddressed sin that
condemns us. But God *can* take away our guilt. For Isaiah that meant
a coal from the altar. The altar was the place of sacrifice. A person's
guilt was symbolically placed on an animal, and the animal died in
their place. Fire in the Old Testament is a picture of God's all-consum-
ing wrath. The punishment for sin was paid by the animal instead of
by the worshipper. It's a symbol, a picture, a promise. It points us to
Jesus, the perfect sacrifice, who takes away the sin of the world.

Send me

Isaiah then hears God saying, "Whom shall I send? And who will
go for us?" and Isaiah responds, "Here am I. Send me!" (**6:8**) He's
not saying, *I'll do you a favour* or *I'm the ideal man for the job*. He's
just said, "I am a man of unclean lips"! But when you've seen the
majesty of God and when you've experienced his **grace**, you cannot
but serve God.

The job that Isaiah gets is not a great one: he's to speak to people
who will refuse to listen! In fact, he's going to make the situation worse.
The more Isaiah speaks, the more opposed to God people will become.
God is going to use Isaiah to harden their hearts, confirm their blindness
and prepare them for judgment (**6:9-10**). Nor is this unique to Isaiah.
Jesus quoted Isaiah 6 to explain why he spoke in **parables** (Matthew
13:10-17). God uses us in the same way. To some our words bring life.
But other people reject our words, and, in doing so, they're confirmed
in their judgment—both their judgment against Christ and God's judg-
ment against them. Paul says, "For we are to God the pleasing aroma of
Christ among those who are being saved and those who are perishing.
To the one we are an aroma that brings death; to the other, an aroma
that brings life" (2 Corinthians 2:15-16).

But people are not hardened for ever. Isaiah asks, "For how long, Lord?" in **6:11** and is told it will be "until the cities lie ruined": that is, until Israel and Judah have been defeated and exiled. Then Isaiah 6 ends with the words, "The holy seed will be the stump in the land" (**6:13**). In other words, there is something left in the land that is alive— even if only just. It's a theme that re-emerges in Isaiah 11:1, where a shoot will come from the stump of Jesse—the father of King David, Israel's greatest king. So a chapter that began with the death of one king ends with the promise of another. Out of the wastes of the impending judgment, the promised messianic King will come.

So it is that later, in Isaiah's song of the suffering Servant (52:13 – 53:12) we read, "For what they were not told, they will see, and what they have not heard, they will understand" (52:15). It's the exact opposite of **6:9**: "Be ever hearing, but never understanding; be ever seeing, but never perceiving". Isaiah will encounter people who hear but do not understand. But one day there will be people who have not heard but do understand. We find the same idea in 65:1, where God says, "I revealed myself to those who did not ask for me; I was found by those who did not seek me".

God is talking about us. We weren't on some great quest for God. God found us. Even if you can remember a period when you were searching for God, it's because God himself put that longing in your heart. Left to themselves, "no one calls on [God's] name," says Isaiah in 64:7. But God has not left us to ourselves. In his grace he sought us out. We were deaf to God's voice and blind to his glory (**6:9-10**). Even those who encountered the glory of God in the person of Christ were blind to that glory (John 12:37-41, quoting Isaiah 53:1 and **6:10**). But the Holy Spirit opened our ears and eyes to recognise the glory of God in the face of Jesus Christ.

What are we to do in response to this vision of God's holiness?

First, we say, "Woe to me! I am ruined! I am unclean." We stop pretending because we cannot pretend before God. We stop hiding because we cannot hide from God. We stop coming to God pointing to our goodness, service or efforts. It doesn't matter whether you've been a Christian for decades or whether you've never come to God before. Open your eyes to the holiness of God and cry out in humility, "Woe to me! I deserve to be cursed." The aim is not to make you miserable. Instead, this is an opportunity for true cleansing. Cry out to God and he will cleanse you. The fire of his judgment that fell on Christ will touch your lips and life with purifying power. Today you may feel, "I don't really want to engage with my sin or God's holiness." But you're going to have to face God one day. And if you face God cleansed by the blood of Christ, then what you will see will be the love of a Father and "the beauty of the LORD" (Psalm 27:4).

The second thing to note as we think about how we respond to this vision of God's holiness is that there's no room for compromise in his presence. In many situations I'm a "that'll do" kind of person. "It doesn't need to be perfect." "Good enough is good enough." That may be fine for household chores. But the one area where "that'll do" will certainly *not* do is holiness. When it comes to obeying God, there is no room for half measures—not when you see the holiness of God. We need to be ruthless with sin and flee temptation. We need to hear the call to service and respond as Isaiah did: "Here am I. Send me!"

Questions for reflection

1. What experience do you have of being rejected when you have tried to share the message of Christ? What comfort is there in this passage for you?

2. Think about your own journey to faith. As you look back, how can you see that God was the one at work in you the whole time?

3. How will you respond to this vision of holiness today?

2. GOD PROMISES HIS PRESENCE

FOCUS: ISAIAH 8:19 – 9:7

What's the biggest threat we face at the moment? The fallout of a global pandemic, perhaps. Or climate change or intergenerational inequality. Or shifting geopolitical power. How do you see your personal future? Perhaps you face growing health issues or you worry how you'll manage in retirement. For many people the future feels *gloomy*.

For God's people the future looked gloomy. In Isaiah 7 King Ahaz is king of Judah, and he has a problem. After the death of King Solomon in 931 the nation had divided into two. The two southern tribes of Israel's twelve tribes formed the nation of Judah (the nation ruled by King Ahaz). The ten northern tribes were known as Israel or Ephraim. Israel or Ephraim has formed an alliance with Aram. Aram (also known as Syria, though this is somewhat misleading because Aram does not wholly map onto modern-day Syria) was a neighbouring kingdom to the north of Israel. Together Ephraim and Aram have ganged up against Judah (7:1-2).

So Isaiah says to King Ahaz, "Be careful, keep calm and don't be afraid" (7:3-4). It's the eighth century BC equivalent of the famous British wartime poster: "Keep Calm and Carry On". In other words, trust in God and everything will be all right (7:5-9). Isaiah even invites King Ahaz to ask for a sign (7:10). Perhaps Isaiah can see that Ahaz is uncertain, and so he says, in effect, *Let God reassure you. Before you bet your future on the LORD, let the LORD give you a sign.*

Ahaz replies, "I will not put the LORD to the test" (7:12). It sounds rather pious. But basically Ahaz is saying, *Thanks, but no thanks. I'm going to look for help elsewhere. I'm going to do a deal with Assyria.* So God gives Ahaz a sign that he's not looking for: "Therefore the Lord himself will give you a sign: the virgin will conceive and give birth to a son, and will call him Immanuel" (7:12-14). It's a famous Christmas promise. But originally it was a word of judgment. Ahaz is a descendant of King David, and God had promised David that his line would always rule over God's people. So it looks like God needs Ahaz so God can keep his promise to David. But here God is saying, *I can bring the reign of David's godless sons to an end and then start again with a virgin.* King Ahaz thinks he can do without God, but it's God who can do without Ahaz. God can judge the house of David and still fulfil his promise to David by raising up a king from a virgin. Yes, God will defeat Israel and Aram (7:16). But God will also judge Judah (7:17).

> Jesus will come, and he will be called Immanuel.

The promised boy will grow up eating honey and curds (7:15). It's the food of poverty—a sign that Judah's economy will collapse (7:18-25). So Jesus will come, and he will be called "Immanuel": God with us. But before this happens, both Israel and Judah will have experienced defeat and exile.

Then Isaiah himself has a son, and this baby boy is another sign of judgment. Isaiah calls him "Maher-Shalal-Hash-Baz", which means "quick to the plunder, swift to the spoil" (8:1). It's not what you want to hear shouted from the back door at meal times! In the lifetime of Maher-Shalal-Hash-Baz the Assyrians would defeat the two nations currently threatening Judah—Ephraim and Aram (symbolised by their respective capital cities, Samaria and Damascus, 8:1-4). But don't rejoice, says Isaiah, because the Assyrian "floodwaters" will sweep over Judah as well (8:5-8). Judah hoped the Assyrian Empire would deliver them, but Assyria would turn out to be an even bigger threat.

Reader's guide

Isaiah 7 - 8

The southern kingdom of Judah is threatened by the nations of Israel (otherwise known as Ephraim) and Aram. So Isaiah invites King Ahaz to trust in the LORD and offers to send a sign to reassure him (7:1-11). But King Ahaz refuses this, opting instead to make an alliance with Assyria (7:12). So God says he will reboot the Davidic dynasty (7:13-14). Assyria will defeat Israel and Aram (7:15-16), but the Assyrian floodwaters will also sweep over Judah (7:17-25; 8:4-8). The name of Isaiah's child, Maher-Shalal-Hash-Baz, which means "quick to the plunder, swift to the spoil", is a pointer to this disaster (8:1-4). It's not political plots and conspiracies that we should fear but the LORD (8:9-18). Because they reject God, the people instead consult mediums and spiritists, but that road leads only to darkness (8:19-22).

Isaiah 9:1-7

God's judgment leaves the world in darkness (9:1). But light will dawn in the form of a child—a coming King who will reign in peace and justice (9:2-7). It's a promise fulfilled at the birth of Jesus (Luke 1:31-33).

How did people respond to this gloomy outlook? In many ways their responses back then mirror the responses of people today.

Some people took what we might call *the superstitious option.* "When someone tells you to consult mediums and spiritists," says **8:19**, "who whisper and mutter, should not a people enquire of their God? Why consult the dead on behalf of the living?" People want guidance for this life or reassurance about the life to come. And so they go to mediums. There are more mediums in Italy than Roman Catholic priests! The obvious person to turn to is God—the eternal God, who exists outside of time, and the Lord of history, who shapes the future. But what people hear from God is "the testimony of warning" (**8:20**). So they prefer to look elsewhere. "Tell us pleasant things," they say in 30:10: "Prophesy illusions".

But as Isaiah says, "Why consult the dead on behalf of the living?" (**8:19**). Our biggest threat is death. That's the fate that none of us can avoid. And the dead are those who have *lost* that battle. By definition they're clearly not the best people to consult! What we need is someone who came back from death—someone who defeated death.

There's another response that Isaiah describes, which today we might call *the rationalist option*. "Distressed and hungry, they will roam through the land", says **8:21**; "when they are famished, they will become enraged and, looking upwards, will curse their king and their God." These people blame God. Why has God let this happen? Today it is common for people to say, "If God is so loving, why does he allow suffering?" Following this line of argument, many people conclude there is no God. But there's an anger that belies their conclusion. They rage against the God who they claim does not exist. "They curse their king and their God."

Here's the problem with this logic. In **8:22** Isaiah says, "Then they will look towards the earth and see only distress and darkness and fearful gloom, and they will be thrust into utter darkness." In **8:21** they look *upwards* and curse God; now in **8:22** they look *outwards* and see only gloom. That's what happens when you take God out of the picture. You're left without any **objective** moral standard. If you take God away, you take justice away with him. For without God there are no objective criteria to judge what is right and wrong. You're left with the survival of the fittest. There's no one to hold people to account. The result is distress and gloom. There's no light of **revelation** and no hope of redemption. Humanity is left to itself, and that is not a happy prospect. So the best we can hope for is to muddle through life without facing a major illness, crime, redundancy or war. But even if people avoid these things, in the end every life ends in *death*.

Light is coming

This is the dark backdrop to the wonderful promises of Isaiah **9:1-7**. Into this distress, darkness and gloom, light is coming:

"Nevertheless, there will be no more gloom for those who were in distress. In the past he humbled the land of Zebulun and the land of Naphtali, but in the future he will honour Galilee of the nations, by the Way of the Sea, beyond the Jordan—

The people walking in darkness
    have seen a great light;
on those living in the land of deep darkness
    a light has dawned." (**9:1-2**)

Zebulun and Naphtali were the two most northerly of the twelve tribes of Israel. So when the Assyrian army came, it came first to Zebulun and Naphtali. The darkness fell on them first.

These regions were already notorious as areas in which the first generation of Israelites in the land had failed to drive out the Canaanites (Judges 1:30, 33). Galilee, too, had a dubious reputation. Twenty Galilean towns had been given to Hiram king of Tyre by Solomon in return for building supplies, but it seems Hiram had been somewhat underwhelmed by what he had received. He nicknamed them "the Land of Kabul" which means "good-for-nothing", a name which the writer of Kings says "they have to this day" (1 Kings 9:10-13). No wonder Isaiah says they were humbled.

But that was "in the past". Now Isaiah contrasts their past with what will happen "in the future". The promise is that a light is coming, and it's going to come to them first. The distress, darkness and gloom with which we ended chapter 8 are going to give way to light. "There will be no more gloom" (**9:1**). "A light has dawned" (**9:2**). Gloom will be replaced by joy. Isaiah **9:3** talks about joy four times:

"You have enlarged the nation
    and increased their *joy*;
they *rejoice* before you
    as people *rejoice* at the harvest,
as warriors *rejoice*
    when dividing the plunder." (Emphasis added)

An end to conflict

Both **9:4** and **9:5** begin "For..." In **9:1-3**, darkness will be replaced by light, and gloom will be replaced by joy. Why? Here are two reasons:

"For as in the day of Midian's defeat,
    you have shattered
the yoke that burdens them,
    the bar across their shoulders,
    the rod of their oppressor.
[For] every warrior's boot used in battle
    and every garment rolled in blood
will be destined for burning,
    will be fuel for the fire." (**9:4-5**)

Reason #1: God is going to end *oppression*—he will shatter "the yoke that burdens them" (**9:4**). All the injustice, exploitation, insecurity, unfair wages and corruption that scar our world will be eradicated. As a result, we will rejoice "as people rejoice at the harvest", because we will enjoy the fruit of our labour (**9:3**).

Reason #2: God is going to end *war*—"every warrior's boot" will be burned (**9:5**). Isaiah is reworking the promise of 2:4, where he talked about swords being beaten into ploughshares and spears into pruning hooks. And we so will rejoice like "warriors ... dividing the plunder" (**9:3**).

Watch any television news programme or read any newspaper and you will readily see what an amazing promise this is. This is unbelievably good news.

But how will it happen? **9:6** also begins "For..." Here's the means by which God will end oppression and war:

"For to us a child is born,
    to us a son is given,
    and the government will be on his shoulders.
And he will be called
    Wonderful Counsellor, Mighty God,
    Everlasting Father, Prince of Peace.

Of the greatness of his government and peace
   there will be no end.
He will reign on David's throne
   and over his kingdom,
establishing and upholding it
   with justice and righteousness
   from that time on and for ever.
The zeal of the LORD Almighty
   will accomplish this." **(9:6-7)**

This is the son promised in Isaiah 7:14 and the son promised to David in 2 Samuel 7:12-14. A king is coming, a new King David (Israel's greatest king), who will reign over God's people in justice and peace. This is Jesus.

The reason why we so often read this passage at Christmas is that its fingerprints are all over the Gospel narratives. In Luke's Gospel we read, "God sent the angel Gabriel to Nazareth, a town in Galilee, to a virgin pledged to be married to a man named Joseph, a descendant of David. The virgin's name was Mary" (Luke 1:26-27). Just so we don't miss the geographical allusion, Luke tells us that Nazareth is a town in Galilee—the place where Isaiah **9:1-2** said light would dawn. Then Luke tells us the angel came to a virgin—just as Isaiah 7:14 had promised. He tells us too that she is a married to a descendant of David—just as Isaiah **9:7** had promised. And the angel hasn't even spoken yet! When he does speak, this is what he says:

"You will conceive and give birth to a son, and you are to call
him Jesus. He will be great and will be called the Son of the
Most High. The Lord God will give him the throne of his father
David, and he will reign over Jacob's descendants for ever; his
kingdom will never end." (Luke 1:31-33)

Isaiah 7:14 says, "The virgin will conceive'; the angel says, "You will conceive." Isaiah **9:6** says, "A child is born … a son is given"; the angel says, "You will give birth to a son". Isaiah **9:7** says, "He will reign on David's throne"; the angel says, "The Lord God will give him the throne of his father David." Isaiah **9:7** says, "He will reign … over his kingdom ... for ever"; the angel says, "He will reign over Jacob's descendants for ever; his kingdom will never end".

Matthew, too, quotes from Isaiah **9:1** in Matthew 4:12-14 to show that this promise is fulfilled by Jesus:

"When Jesus heard that John had been put in prison, he withdrew to Galilee. Leaving Nazareth, he went and lived in Capernaum, which was by the lake in the area of Zebulun and Naphtali—to fulfil what was said through the prophet Isaiah."

Matthew makes the same geographical link. The early ministry of Jesus took place in Galilee. This was where the light first dawned, just as Isaiah had said it would. But, of course, the real point Matthew is making is that the Jesus is the light. He is the one who ends our fear and dispels our gloom.

Questions for reflection

1. How do you tend to respond when things seem gloomy? Where do you recognise yourself in Isaiah 8 and 9?

2. Why is life without God a life of darkness and gloom? How is that borne out in your own experience?

3. What injustices or conflicts do you particularly long to see an end to? How can you pray in the light of this passage?

PART TWO

Isaiah promises a royal child who will end darkness and gloom. It's a pointer to Jesus. But how will Jesus end our darkness? Isaiah says he will end oppression and war. Instead of oppression, he will establish and uphold his kingdom with justice (**9:7b**). Instead of war, his government will bring a peace to which "there will be no end" (**9:7a**). It's all about power. This is not a description of a cute, harmless baby. This is a king. This is *political* language.

- "The *government* will be on his shoulders" (**9:6**).

- "Of the greatness of his *government* and peace there will be no end" (**9:7**).

- "He will *reign* on David's *throne* and over his *kingdom*" (**9:7**; emphasis added).

We can rejoice (**9:3**) becomes God will end oppression (**9:4**) and war (**9:5**) through his king (**9:6**) who will reign for ever (**9:7**).

We're not to spiritualise this—it is a political message. It's the promise of a radically different kind of politics, of a new and better government. The burden of debt will be lifted. The gloom of unemployment will end. The fear of sexual harassment will be gone. The threat of conflict will disappear.

This is what Isaiah promises, and this is what Jesus will deliver. One day Jesus will return to this earth. In the Lord's Prayer we say, "Your kingdom come, your will be done on earth as in heaven." That prayer will be answered when Jesus returns and establishes his government, "upholding it with justice and righteousness from that time on and for ever", as **9:7** says.

You don't need me to tell you that we're not there yet. We still see oppression and injustice every time we turn on the news. Many of us experience it in our own lives. But we got a glimpse of this coming reign of Jesus in his life on earth. There we saw his *power* as he commanded the waves, rebuked sickness, subdued demons, and even defeated death. But we also saw his *justice*. Not only did he exercise authority; he exercised authority "with justice and righteousness", as Isaiah had promised in **9:7**. He fed the poor, denounced hypocrisy, welcomed children, treated prostitutes with dignity and touched lepers. This is our King, and he's coming to reign. He's coming to end our conflict with one another.

Wonderful Counsellor

Isaiah gives us a window onto the reign of King Jesus in the names he ascribes to him:

"And he will be called
Wonderful Counsellor, Mighty God,
Everlasting Father, Prince of Peace." (**9:6**)

The kingdom of Israel got into a mess because they lacked or ignored wise counsel. But Isaiah had promised to restore their counsellors (1:26). Now he promises a wonderful counsellor-king. "Wonderful Counsellor" doesn't just mean a really good counsellor. It's the language of "signs and wonders". It means Jesus has miraculous or supernatural counsel. Isaiah himself elaborates on this in 11:2-4:

"The Spirit of the LORD will rest on him—
the Spirit of wisdom and of understanding,
the Spirit of counsel and of might,
the Spirit of the knowledge and fear of the LORD—
and he will delight in the fear of the LORD.
He will not judge by what he sees with his eyes,
or decide by what he hears with his ears;
but with righteousness he will judge the needy,
with justice he will give decisions for the poor of the earth."

In other words, Jesus has Spirit-enabled insight. As a result, his decisions are just, and his reign is righteous.

Often people benefit from the help of a counsellor, someone who can give them a broader perspective on the emotional problems they face. But Christians have something even more wonderful—our own Wonderful Counsellor, the Lord Jesus Christ. His words are life and health (Proverbs 4:22). The truth he proclaims is the truth that sets us free. His words are like "the first gleam of dawn" (Proverbs 4:18, NLT).

Mighty God

It's hard to know what Isaiah's first hearers thought when they heard the coming King described as "Mighty God". Isaiah says, "A child is born" (**9:6**). This is undoubtedly a human being with a human origin. And yet he's also the Mighty God. Isaiah uses the same phrase in 10:21 to describe how God saves the **remnant** of his people. God himself, in the person of Jesus, has entered our world. In 7:14 and 8:9-10 Isaiah promises that the coming child will be *Immanuel*, "God with us" (Matthew 1:23). God has got involved in our broken world. He didn't look down from above, muttering about the mess we were making of his world. He rolled up his sleeves and got stuck in. God has entered our world to sort it out.

Everlasting Father

At first sight "Everlasting Father" also looks like an odd description, especially as the coming King has just been called "a child" and "a son". It echoes the opening of the book of Isaiah:

"Hear me, you heavens! Listen, earth!
    For the LORD has spoken:
  'I reared children and brought them up,
      but they have rebelled against me.'" (1:2)

God has been a father to his people. He created them, reared them, and cared for them. And now the King is coming to recreate God's people. They are going to be born again as a new people.

Prince of Peace

Finally Jesus is called "Prince of Peace". Isaiah **9:4** says, "… as in the day of Midian's defeat". It's a reference to the time when Gideon defeated the enemies of God's people with just 300 men (Judges 7). Now God is again going to bring peace to his people by defeating their enemies. But this time he's going to do so through just one person.

What are we to do in response to the coming of the King? Isaiah says, "Do not fear what they fear" (8:11-12). We can entrust our lives to him. We can live as those held in his hands. The 4th-century preacher John Chrysostom said, "The peace which comes from a human being is easily destroyed and subject to many changes. But Christ's peace is strong, unshaken, firm, fixed, steadfast, immune to death and unending" (*Demonstrations Against the Pagans* 2.10; cited in Steve A. McKinion (ed.), *Ancient Christian Commentary on Scripture Vol. X*, p 76).

The greater conflict

But Jesus does something even more significant than ending human conflict. Isaiah **9:7** says, "There will be no end" to the peace brought by the Son on David's throne. The son who initially took over from King David was Solomon. His name means "man of peace", and his reign was a golden age for God's people. But it didn't last because Solomon could not sort out the real problem. Our ultimate threat is not political oppression or war. Our ultimate threat is God himself: his holiness and justice. To understand the fullness of what Isaiah is promising in chapter 9, we need to read it in the light of his warning in 8:12-13:

"Do not call conspiracy
    everything this people calls a conspiracy;
do not fear what they fear,
    and do not dread it.
The LORD Almighty is the one you are to regard as holy,
    he is the one you are to fear,
    he is the one you are to dread."

The real issue was not whether Aram, Israel, Judah or Assyria had the biggest army or the healthiest economy. The real issue was God. Behind all the machinations of ancient geopolitics, God was judging the nations. What happened to these nations nearly three millennia ago was a sign and pointer to the judgment facing all humanity.

We live in a world of fear—of conspiracies, half-truths and fake news, all fed by internet rumours. Our fears may be domestic. We may worry that what we're eating is unsafe or that what we're prescribed will make things worse. The distortions of the media may make us fearful of crime or worried about the safety of our children. The political discourse fuels people's fears of immigrants and refugees. Or we fear Russian interference and Chinese expansionism. We fear super-bugs and computer viruses. It's easy to get caught up in these conspiracies—to "fear what they fear" (8:12).

> Our ultimate threat is not political oppression or war. It is God himself.

The point is not that these are empty threats. Some paranoid conspiracies turn out be true! The point is they're not the *real* threat, not ultimately. Isaiah says, "The LORD Almighty ... is the one you are to dread". As we saw in Isaiah 6, it is God's holiness that threatens our ruin. "He will be a holy place," says 8:14, and "a stone that causes people to stumble". The day is coming when we will all face God. That's our real problem.

Yet at the birth of Jesus, the angels proclaimed, "Glory to God in the highest heaven, and on earth peace to those on whom his favour rests" (Luke 2:14). They were not simply declaring the end of human conflict. They were declaring peace with God. The God we have made our enemy was coming to earth to offer peace to all who would receive it. He came in the person of his Son to die in our place, making reparation for the wrongs we have done. Colossians 1:21-22 says:

"You were [God's] enemies, separated from him by your evil thoughts and actions. Yet now he has reconciled you to himself through the death of Christ in his physical body. As a result, he has brought you into his own presence, and you are holy and blameless as you stand before him without a single fault." (NLT)

I was recently in Sunderland, north-east England, and visited Monkwearmouth, the site of an early Anglo-Saxon monastery. Thirteen centuries ago it was the home to the Venerable Bede at a time when the north-east of England was the cultural and theological powerhouse of Europe. Here's what Bede says about Isaiah 9:

"Surely the entire divinely arranged plan of our Redeemer's [coming] in the flesh is the reconciliation of the world—it was for this purpose that he became **incarnate**, for this he suffered, for this he was raised from the dead—that he might lead us, who had incurred God's anger by sinning, back to God's peace by his act of reconciliation. Hence he was rightly given the name 'Father of the world to come' and 'Prince of peace'."
(*Homilies on the Gospels* 2.9; cited in Steve A. McKinion (ed.), *Ancient Christian Commentary on Scripture Vol. X*, p 73.)

Today we can be reconciled with God and live at peace with God through Jesus. "I will put my trust in him," says Isaiah in 8:17. Today we look forward to the coming reign of Jesus, and as we do so our gloomy future becomes a bright future.

Questions for reflection

1. How does this portrait of Jesus change your perspective on political or social issues?

2. What aspect of his character feels particularly relevant to your life or the life of your church right now?

3. What do people around you fear? How could you show that you believe in a God who is bigger than those fears?

3. GOD ANOINTS HIS KING

FOCUS: ISAIAH 11:1 - 12:6

In chapter 9 Isaiah describes how God is going to use the Assyrian Empire to judge the northern kingdom of Israel. It is a sobering chapter. In 9:8-12 Israel think they can rebuild after judgment, but they're going to be devoured. So in verse 12 Isaiah says, "Yet for all this, his anger is not turned away, his hand is still upraised".

The word "upraised" is the word that was used in the story of the exodus to describe God's hand being "outstretched" in judgment against Egypt (Exodus 6:6). Isaiah says there is going to be a new exodus, but this time God's hand will not be stretched out *for* Israel but *against* Israel. Even after the northern kingdom has been devoured, God's anger is not turned away.

In 9:13-17 God will take away their leaders and prophets because everyone is ungodly. But even this will not be enough. After corrupt leaders have been removed, still Isaiah says in 9:17, "Yet for all this, his anger is not turned away, his hand is still upraised".

In 9:18-21 the people will be consumed both by the fires of their own wickedness (9:18) and by the fire of God's wrath (9:19). But even after God has **purged** his people, still Isaiah says in 9:21, "Yet for all this, his anger is not turned away, his hand is still upraised".

In 10:1-4 Isaiah says that, because of their injustice, there will be nowhere to hide when God judges. Judgment will come, and no one will escape. But even after this has happened, still Isaiah says in 10:4, "Yet for all this, his anger is not turned away, his hand is still upraised".

Four times Isaiah tells us that God's anger is not turned away.

A tool in God's hands

Then Isaiah turns his attention to Assyria itself (10:12, 24-25). God calls Assyria "the rod of my anger" (10:5). "I send him against a godless nation, I dispatch him against a people who anger me" (10:6). In other words, Assyria is a tool being used by God.

It can seem as if history is out of control or a series of random events or controlled by evil men. But God uses the nations to achieve his purposes.

But that is not how Assyria sees it (10:8-11). In 10:13-14 Assyria says, "By the strength of my hand I have done this, and by my wisdom, because I have understanding". The tool thinks it is the master!

"Does the axe raise itself above the person who swings it,
    or the saw boast against the one who uses it?
As if a rod were to wield the person who lifts it up,
    or a club brandish the one who is not wood!" (10:15)

Moreover, although God is using Assyria to judge, the motives of the Assyrians are far from good.

"But this is not what he intends,
    this is not what he has in mind;
his purpose is to destroy,
    to put an end to many nations." (10:7)

So, because Assyria exceeds its divine **mandate**, God will judge it. "When the Lord has finished all his work against Mount Zion and Jerusalem, he will say, 'I will punish the king of Assyria for the wilful pride of his heart and the haughty look in his eyes'" (10:12). Nothing will be left standing. This is the message of 10:16-19, 23 and 26-34.

In 10:17 Isaiah says, "The Light of Israel will become a fire, their Holy One a flame; in a single day it will burn and consume [Assyria's] thorns and his briers". Perhaps you've seen the aftermath of a forest fire or the clearing of heather on the moors. You're left with nothing but blackened earth. That is the image here.

Imagine sending a child into a vast forest to catalogue all the trees. It's a ridiculous idea. But the fire of God's judgment will be so complete that in 10:19 Isaiah says, "The remaining trees of [Assyria's] forests will be so few that a child could write them down."

In 10:33 Isaiah uses a related image to speak of Assyria's defeat. This time, instead of fire bringing destruction, God is likened to a lumberjack:

"See, the Lord, the LORD Almighty,
> will lop off the boughs with great power.
The lofty trees will be felled,
> the tall ones will be brought low."

I was recently walking in the Welsh mountains, and there was an area of pine forest that had been cleared. The trees had been planted close together so that nothing grew between them. All there was on the floor of the wood were dead pine needles. Now that the trees had all been felled, all that was left was a barren stretch of dead tree stumps.

We need to pause at this point and take in the scene. As far as the eye can see there's just blackened earth. Or think of the trenches after the First World War—acres of bare mud and blasted tree stumps. Think of the war-time paintings of Paul Nash. If you are unfamiliar with his work, do an image search on the internet. He powerfully portrays the devastation left after battle.

Then Isaiah sees something in the mud, the death and the emptiness. In **11:1** he says, "A shoot will come up from the stump of Jesse; from his roots a Branch will bear fruit". Jesse was the father of King David, Israel's greatest king. So the stump of Jesse is David's family. A new David is coming.

The northern kingdom of Israel was destroyed, as Isaiah said it would be in chapter 9. The Assyrian Empire was destroyed, as Isaiah said it would be in chapter 10. But somehow little Judah, battered and bruised, continued. A remnant among God's people would survive (10:20-22). And from that remnant would come a new King—a new King David.

The first king of Israel, King Saul, rejected God. So God sent the prophet Samuel to anoint a replacement. Israelite kings were not crowned. Instead they were anointed with oil. So the king was known as "the anointed one". The Hebrew word for this is "messiah" and the Greek is "christ". David was the christ (small "c"). He was God's anointed king. Outwardly the king was anointed with oil. But what really mattered was being anointed with the Spirit of the LORD. The account of David being anointed comes to a climax in this way: "So Samuel took the horn of oil and anointed him in the presence of his brothers, and from that day on the Spirit of the LORD came powerfully upon David" (1 Samuel 16:13). That is what equipped a man to rescue and rule God's people. David went on to become Israel's greatest king. He defeated Israel's enemies and gave the people rest in the land. But his successors were not of the same calibre. Even David himself did not finish well. In the end, the kingdom was lost, and David's successors became puppets under Babylonian rule. The house of Jesse was reduced to a stump. And that might have been the end of the story.

But from that stump would come a new King—anointed not with oil but with the Spirit of the LORD. The Spirit would equip him to rescue and rule God's people. It is almost as if Isaiah imagines the prophet Samuel again making the journey to the house of Jesse to anoint a new king. Perhaps Isaiah thought it would be King Hezekiah—the great reforming king of Judah. But although Hezekiah was a good king in many ways, his reign would end in failure (Isaiah 39:1-8). No, only Jesus fulfils the expectations of God's people and the promises of God's prophets. And what does King Jesus do? What is his reign like? That is the theme of Isaiah 11.

A reign of justice

One of the key reasons why God judges Israel is that they "deprive the poor of their rights and withhold justice from the oppressed of my people" (10:2). Now compare this with Isaiah's description of King Jesus: "With righteousness he will judge the needy, with justice he will give decisions for the poor of the earth" (**11:4**). During his life on earth Jesus was not a judge or a king. He had no political power. But we get a flavour of his coming reign in his earthly ministry. He fed the hungry, healed the sick, denounced injustice and condemned corruption. He did not prey on widows as Israel's leaders did in 10:2; instead he went to their aid, as he did, for example, in the town of Nain (Luke 7:11-15).

> We find it hard to deliver justice. But Jesus judges with supernatural insight.

But it is not just that Jesus is committed to justice. After all, many good people are committed to justice. But we find it hard to deliver it, because our knowledge and powers are limited. Those of you who get competing claims from your children know this. "I had it first," says one. "No, you didn't," says another. Who can decide? And these are just trivial domestic disputes. How about intricate court cases or complex policy decisions or competing social demands? The good news is that Jesus does not simply judge "by what he sees with his eyes" (**11:3**). He judges with supernatural insight (Luke 11:17; John 2:25; Romans 2:16) because he is anointed with the Spirit of the LORD:

"The Spirit of the LORD will rest on him—
    the Spirit of wisdom and of understanding,
    the Spirit of counsel and of might,
    the Spirit of the knowledge and fear of the LORD." (**11:2**)

This describes Jesus. When Jesus was baptised, the Holy Spirit descended on him. Jesus was anointed—not with oil like Israelite kings but with the Spirit of God. Luke then tells us that Jesus conducted his ministry "in the power of the Spirit" (Luke 4:14). In other words, Jesus conducted his ministry with wisdom, understanding, counsel and might. Through the Spirit, Jesus is able to turn his commitment to justice into reality.

Think about what this means for the reign of Jesus over your life. He cares for you with wisdom, understanding, counsel and might. We can sometimes feel misunderstood, especially by those in authority over us. But Jesus understands you better than you understand yourself. He never puts a foot wrong or speaks a word out of place as he counsels you. As you read his word or hear it preached, Jesus himself is shaping your life with perfect, Spirit-enabled wisdom.

Notice, too, "he will delight in the fear of the LORD" (**11:3**). What perverts human justice? Often it is the fear of man. Whether it is a child in the playground or a high-court judge serving under a tyrant, people often do the wrong thing because they fear upsetting those with power. We long to be accepted, and we're terrified of being rejected, so we do what we must to fit in. But not Jesus. What determines his behaviour is the fear of the LORD. In other words, there is only one person Jesus will please at any cost—and that is his heavenly Father. It is this which liberates him to bring justice to the poor.

The earth renewed

In **11:6** Isaiah says:

"The wolf will live with the lamb,
    the leopard will lie down with the goat,
  the calf and the lion and the **yearling** together;
    and a little child will lead them."

It is difficult to know whether ultimately this will be literal or symbolic. But the point is clear: under the reign of Jesus, hostilities will end. His kingdom will be a kingdom of peace (as we saw in 9:2-7). "They will neither harm nor destroy on all my holy mountain," says **11:9**.

Isaiah is looking back in order to look forward. He takes us back to the **Garden of Eden**. He describes the coming reign of Jesus as the restoration of paradise. Here is Jesus, the new Adam, reigning over creation in peace and prosperity. Or again Isaiah says in **11:9**, "The earth will be filled with the knowledge of the LORD as the waters cover the sea". This is the language of Genesis 1. When God first made humanity, he told them to "be fruitful", to "fill the earth and subdue it", to rule over the animals (Genesis 1:28). Jesus is putting that mandate back on track.

This explains a rather enigmatic comment in Mark's Gospel. Jesus has been baptised and anointed by the Spirit. Then we read, "At once the Spirit sent him out into the wilderness ... *He was with the wild animals,* and angels attended him" (Mark 1:12-13, emphasis added). As Mark describes Jesus with the wild animals, he almost certainly has Isaiah 11 in mind. Here is God's King subduing creation—just as Adam should have done, just as Isaiah had promised, just as we will do when Christ returns.

Questions for reflection

1. How do you think you would have responded to Isaiah's words if you had been living during his times?

2. How do you respond to the idea that by his Spirit Jesus is even now shaping your life with wisdom?

3. What light does Isaiah 11:6-9 shed on the created world? What do you think our attitude should be towards it? Why?

PART TWO

Whenever I get to the end of a tube of toothpaste, I carefully roll up the tube to squeeze out the last bit of toothpaste. And that's how my evangelism so often feels. I wrap myself up in guilt until a tiny bit of Jesus squeezes out. What I would like to be like is a champagne bottle which has just gone off with a bang and champagne is pouring out, down the bottle, up someone's arm, into a glass, onto the floor—fizzing and bubbling out. I wonder which you are—toothpaste or champagne? In Isaiah 9 – 11, Isaiah is seeing such a wonderful vision of God's coming salvation that he is left fizzing with praise to God—praise that bubbles out to the nations.

We see in the ministry of Jesus a glimpse of the coming reign that Isaiah promises. What will the kingdom of Jesus be like when he returns? It will be a kingdom of peace, the restoration of humanity and the renewal of creation.

Gathering people

In **11:10-16** Isaiah describes who it is who will enjoy this glorious reign. In **11:15-16** he describes a new exodus—a key theme that recurs throughout Isaiah's ministry:

"The LORD will dry up
    the gulf of the Egyptian sea;
with a scorching wind he will sweep his hand
    over the River Euphrates.
He will break it up into seven streams
    so that anyone can cross over in sandals.
There will be a highway for the remnant of his people
    that is left from Assyria,
as there was for Israel
    when they came up from Egypt."

Here is a clear reference back to the exodus from Egypt under Moses. After Pharaoh had been forced by the ten plagues to let the Israelites go free from their slavery, he changed his mind and sent his army to recapture them. The Israelites found themselves caught between the oncoming army and the waters of the Red Sea. But Exodus 14 describes how God sent a miraculous wind. The word "wind" is the same word as "Spirit" in Hebrew, suggesting that God himself in the person of his Spirit came to rescue his people. This Spirit-wind parted the sea so that God's people could walk through it. When the Egyptian army tried to follow them, the waters folded back over and they were all drowned, leaving God's people safe on the other side.

Now Isaiah promises that God will do it again. Just as he parted the Red Sea, so he will again send his Spirit-wind to create a highway through the sea. Except this time he is going to create a highway through both the Egyptian sea and the Euphrates River. These were the two great bodies of water to the south and to the north of Israel (**11:11**). We need these routes because God's people are going to come home from every direction—"from the four quarters of the earth" (**11:12**).

> At the Red Sea, God came to rescue his people. Now Isaiah promises that God will do it again.

And not just Israel. In **11:10** Isaiah says, "In that day the **Root of Jesse** will stand as a banner for the peoples; the nations will rally to him, and his resting place will be glorious". In **11:11** Isaiah lists the nations from every direction—the extent of his known world. "He will raise a banner from the nations" (**11:12**). Think of a tour guide holding up a brightly coloured umbrella so everyone can follow her. Jesus has raised a banner so everyone can rally to him. And that banner is us! That is what we are doing in the mission of the church. We hold up the gospel so all Christ's people can see their way home through the chaos of life.

"Resting-place" in **11:10** does not mean "grave" as it often does today. It means "home"—the place where you relax. When humanity rebelled against God, we were cast out to the east of Eden, and an angel with a sword was put in place to prevent us returning (Genesis 3:24). When Cain killed his brother he was sent "east of Eden"—further east, further from home (4:16). Cain became a "restless wanderer" (4:14). And that has been humanity's plight ever since. We are restless wanderers, never quite feeling at home. But now Jesus invites to come home to relax in him and through him.

Reader's guide

Isaiah 9:8 - 10:4

God is going to use the Assyrian Empire to judge the northern kingdom of Israel (also known as Ephraim or personified as **Jacob***). The refrain is "Yet for all this, his anger is not turned away, his hand is still upraised" (9:12, 17, 21; 10:4).*

Isaiah 10:5-34

The pagan kingdom of Assyria is described as a tool in God's hands to destroy the northern kingdom of Israel and judge the southern kingdom of Judah (10:5-11). But the Assyrians boasts in their power (10:12-14), so God will destroy Assyria (10:15-19). God promises that a remnant from among his people will return through a new exodus (10:20-34).

Isaiah 11

Isaiah promises a coming King who, empowered by the Spirit, will rule in justice and peace (11:1-9). The King will gather God's people from all nations through a new exodus (11:10-16). It is a promise fulfilled in the coming reign of King Jesus.

Isaiah 12

In response to the promise of a coming King in chapter 11, Isaiah sings a song of praise which calls on us to declare the name of the LORD to all nations.

God's anger hangs over us

But there is a big problem at the heart of this vision—a problem Isaiah flagged up in chapter 9. As we have seen, four times Isaiah declared: "Yet for all this, his anger is not turned away, his hand is still upraised" (9:12, 17, 21; 10:4). It seems there is no end to God's anger against sin.

And if Isaiah were here today, he would look across history and across our world; he would look over your life and into your heart, and he would say:

"His anger is not turned away, his hand is still upraised."

Perhaps you try so hard to please God, to please other people, to prove yourself, and yet, no matter how hard you try, you always seem to fall short. Someone is disappointed.

And "his anger is not turned away".

So you try to make amends. You fill your life with activity—you come to church, say your prayers, share your faith. Or maybe you self-harm, punishing yourself for your wrongdoing. But whatever you do, it never feels enough.

For "his anger is not turned away".

God's anger falls on Christ

So the promise of a reign of justice sounds like bad news. We all want justice. The problem is that we are all guilty. So when justice comes, it comes bringing judgment against us. The coming of God's King will mean the destruction of God's enemies. But then Isaiah says:

"In that day you will say:
'I will praise you, LORD.
   Although you were angry with me,
your anger has turned away
   and you have comforted me.'" (**12:1**, emphasis added)

Four times Isaiah has said "his anger is not turned away" (9:12, 17, 21; 10:4). Each time the words have fallen like a hammer blow against our vain hopes or like a bell tolling our doom. But *now* Isaiah says, "Your anger *has* turned away". This is because when King Jesus came:

"He was pierced for our transgressions,
    he was crushed for our iniquities;
  the punishment that brought us peace was on him,
    and by his wounds we are healed." (53:5)

Isaiah says that when the Messiah comes, "he will strike the earth with the rod of his mouth; with the breath of his lips he will slay the wicked" (**11:4**). When did that happen in the ministry of Jesus? When did Jesus slay the wicked? When did God's judgment fall? The answer is: at the cross. God's judgment fell on the King himself. "The LORD himself," says **12:2**, "he has become my salvation". Salvation is not simply something God *does*. Salvation is something God has become! God in the person of Jesus has become the sacrifice. God's anger has fallen, but he turned it away from us (**12:1**) and directed in onto himself in the person of Jesus. The result for us is comfort. "You have comforted me," says **12:1**.

Toothpaste or champagne?

The second half of **12:2** quotes Exodus 15:2, part of the song sung by Moses after the first exodus. Just as the first exodus was celebrated in song (Exodus 15), so the new exodus leads to a new song. "I will praise you, LORD," says Isaiah in **12:1**. What happens next? In **12:4-6** Isaiah says:

"In that day you will say:
  'Give praise to the LORD, proclaim his name;
    make known among the nations what he has done,
    and proclaim that his name is exalted.
  Sing to the LORD, for he has done glorious things;
    let this be known to all the world.
  Shout aloud and sing for joy, people of **Zion**,
    for great is the Holy One of Israel among you.'"

Is Isaiah talking about worship or mission in these verses? When we see the salvation of God in Jesus, do we burst into song or do we burst out of the door? The answer is both. Mission is worship and worship is mission. Mission is God's people extolling his worth to the nations. If you truly think something is worthy, you want to tell everyone about it.

This changes the way we think about worship, and it changes the way we think about mission. Our worship cannot be inward-looking. We gather each Sunday to retune our hearts so that we worship Christ as living sacrifices throughout the week (Romans 12:1). The shape of our meetings should propel us outwards. When we gather together on a Sunday, we "draw water from the wells of salvation", as **12:3** puts it. But this then fills us with songs of joy that we proclaim to the world (**12:5-6**). People who worship God and do not evangelise are not really worshipping God. They are just enjoying the music. If your heart is filled with the joy of salvation, then you will want to "proclaim that his name is exalted" (**12:4**).

This also changes the way we think about mission. Notice how Isaiah aligns the commands (**12:4-6**): "Give praise", "proclaim", "make known", "proclaim", "sing", "let this be known", "shout aloud", "sing for joy". Our evangelism is so often done out of a sense of guilt. You can make any Christian feel guilty by asking whether they do enough evangelism. But there is no sign of guilt here. Indeed, the guilt was all taken away in **12:1**. Instead, Isaiah's call to mission is fuelled by joy (**12:6**). Is it worship or is it evangelism? The two have merged!

Perhaps some of us need to spend less time thinking about evangelism and more time thinking about Jesus. Perhaps we need to spend more time together drawing water from the wells of salvation (**12:3**). We need to rediscover our enthusiasm for Jesus. Then perhaps, instead of being like empty toothpaste tubes, we will be like bottles of champagne, fizzing with excitement about Jesus. When the opportunity comes... Psssh!

Questions for reflection

1. In what ways do you feel restless or as if in exile? What help does Jesus offer?

2. How does Isaiah 12 challenge your view of worship? How does it challenge your view of evangelism?

3. What does it inspire you to go and do?

4. GOD RULES THE NATIONS

FOCUS: ISAIAH 14

"Reach for the stars; climb every mountain higher … follow your heart's desire." So spoke the great prophets of our age, the pop group S Club 7. They were popular with my daughter—at least, they were when she was seven. The lyrics do capture a common trait of human nature. We long to reach for the stars. We want to be top of the league, top of the class, top of the tree, best in show. We climb the career ladder or clamber up the property ladder. We want to rise.

Perhaps we feel that desire because we know we're *fallen*. We're trying to regain the glory we once had. We were made in the image of God to reflect his glory in the world. But we rejected God and came tumbling down. And ever since we have tried to scramble back up to the top. But now we do it without God. Not content to reflect God's glory, we want to establish our own glory. And so, as S Club 7 go on to say, we have "gotta keep moving … gotta keep building". It's a relentless and exhausting endeavour that leaves us restless and anxious. The message of Isaiah 13 – 23 is that it is futile. Human glory is fleeting and temporary.

Isaiah 13 – 23 is a collection of prophecies addressed to the nations, perhaps drawn together from different points in Isaiah's life. The sequence begins with a description of the downfall of the Babylonian Empire (13:1 – **14:2**). A hundred years or so after Isaiah's ministry, the Babylonian Empire to the north-east of Judah (in modern-day Iraq) replaced the Assyrian Empire as the regional superpower and eventually destroyed Jerusalem, carrying her inhabitants away into exile. But Babylon would not be the last word in history. God was going to "destroy the sinners within it" (13:9), allowing a distressing orgy of violence (13:15-16). Those who remained would be left "like sheep without a shepherd" (13:14), while the land would be taken over by desert creatures (13:20-22).

Although Isaiah says that another regional superpower, the Medes, would do this (13:17-18), it is ultimately *God's* judgment. It is "from the Almighty" (13:6-8; **14:5**). The Medes would come at God's summons (13:2-3). "The LORD Almighty is mustering an army for war," says 13:4. This is how the fall of Babylon is described:

"The stars of heaven and their constellations
　　will not show their light.
The rising sun will be darkened
　　and the moon will not give its light …
Therefore I will make the heavens tremble;
　　and the earth will shake from its place
at the **wrath** of the LORD Almighty,
　　in the day of his burning anger." (13:10, 13)

Isaiah is not describing the end of the world. Kings were portrayed as stars. Today we say, "His star has fallen", and we speak of "earth-shattering" events. The fall of Babylon would be an earth-shattering event. "I will punish the world for its evil, the wicked for their sins," says 13:11.

Two centuries or so later, the defeat of Babylon led to the return of the Jews from exile under **Ezra** and **Nehemiah**. This is what Isaiah describes in **14:1-2**:

"The LORD will have compassion on Jacob;
　　once again he will choose Israel
　　and will settle them in their own land."

This resettlement would take place under the Persian Empire, which replaced the Babylonian Empire as the regional superpower. That is why Isaiah predicts the return from exile at the same time as predicting the defeat of Babylon—events that would take place some 200 years in the future. The story is told in Daniel 5. The king who made Babylon an empire was King Nebuchadnezzar. It was Nebuchadnezzar who defeated Judah and took their leaders into exile, including the young Daniel. 70 years on, Daniel is in his eighties, and Nebuchadnezzar's grandson, Belshazzar, is now the ruler of Babylon. Belshazzar gives a great banquet with 1,000 guests—that is a lot of catering! In the middle of the feasting, Belshazzar decides to get the gold and silver goblets that Nebuchadnezzar had looted from God's temple so his guests can toast the Babylonian gods. In the middle of all this, "suddenly the fingers of a human hand appeared and wrote on the plaster of the wall" (Daniel 5:5). At this the king's "face turned pale and he was so frightened that his legs became weak and his knees were knocking" (5:6). None of the astrologers can make any sense of the writing. So Daniel is called out of retirement and he says:

"This is the inscription that was written:

MENE, MENE, TEKEL, PARSIN

Here is what these words mean:

Mene: God has numbered the days of your reign and brought it to an end.

Tekel: You have been weighed on the scales and found wanting.

Peres: Your kingdom is divided and given to the Medes and Persians." (5:25-28)

Belshazzar tries to shower Daniel with gifts, but Daniel is not interested (5:29). He is over 80 years old. What good are they to him? Besides which, Belshazzar's wealth is about to be stripped away, for even as this conversation takes place, the Medes are entering the city. "That very night Belshazzar, king of the Babylonians, was slain" (5:30).

You can imagine that banquet of 1,000 people thrown into turmoil as news of the attack circulates—everyone running for their lives. In the middle of all the chaos stands Daniel, an old man, thanking God for answering his prayers, seeing God's sovereignty in action, musing on the fragility of human glory and the folly of human pride. And perhaps his mind went to Isaiah 14. For while Isaiah 13 predicts what will happen, Isaiah 14 *interprets* what will happen. What do we learn?

Glory rots away

Isaiah gives God's people a taunt to sing when Babylonian oppression comes to an end (**14:3-8**). "The realm of the dead below," says Isaiah in **14:9**, "is all astir to meet you at your coming". The dead are waiting to receive us. Isaiah imagines Belshazzar's arrival. In **14:10** other kings rise to say, "You also have become weak, as we are; you have become like us". Every great king becomes a dead king, and every mighty man becomes a weak man. Throughout history people have conspired and fought to gain power. And every single one of them loses that power when they die. We do the same now as much as ever—in nations, in workplaces, in homes—and in the end it is all in vain. In the end everyone comes to nothing. Why risk so much, why hurt so much, why envy so much for what does not last?

Isaiah says, "All your pomp has been brought down to the grave, along with the noise of your harps; maggots are spread out beneath you and worms cover you" (**14:11**). It's a very powerful image. The person who was once covered in the finest clothes is now covered in worms. A face that once radiated glamour is now being eaten by maggots. "The pride and glory of the Babylonians, says 13:19, "will be overthrown by God".

Again, nothing has changed. We still work hard to look beautiful. We spend hours in the gym. We buy new clothes. We adopt the latest diet. We idolise the beautiful people. But everyone looks the same after death. The person whose beauty you envy will one day be food for maggots. We don't need the Bible to tell us this. It just takes a moment's reflection. The people in your neighbourhood will (at best) grow old, and 100 per cent of them will die.

Status tumbles down

In **14:12-15** the king of Babylon is pictured as a star:

"How you have fallen from heaven,
   morning star, son of the dawn!
You have been cast down to the earth,
   you who once laid low the nations!
You said in your heart,
   'I will ascend to the heavens ...
   I will make myself like the Most High.'
But you are brought down to the realm of the dead,
   to the depths of the pit."

The king of Babylon reached for the stars, but now his star has fallen. Today we still talk about film stars and sports stars. We emulate the "heights" to which they have "risen". We want to "rise above" our problems and "climb" the career ladder. It is all the language of ascending. We are trying to reverse our fall from glory. So we "reach for the stars".

King Belshazzar's grandfather, Nebuchadnezzar, had tried to reach heaven itself, making divine claims. And so God stripped him of his sanity. For several years he lived like a beast, until eventually he acknowledged that God is God. And Daniel reminds King Belshazzar of this when he interprets the writing on the wall:

"The Most High God gave your father Nebuchadnezzar sovereignty and greatness and glory and splendour ... But when his heart became arrogant and hardened with pride, he was deposed from his royal throne and stripped of his glory. He was driven away from people and given the mind of an animal ... until he acknowledged that the Most High God is sovereign over all kingdoms on earth ...

"But you, Belshazzar, his son, have not humbled yourself, though you knew all this. Instead, you have set yourself up against the Lord of heaven." (Daniel 5:18-23)

This is exactly what Isaiah predicted Babylon's king would do in **14:13-14**: "I will raise my throne above the stars of God … I will make myself like the Most High." And now Daniel says, "You have set yourself up against the Lord of heaven".

> The point is this: no matter how far your star rises, in the end you are brought down to the pit.

Belshazzar was not the first to reach for the stars. Satan tried to take God's place. There may well be echoes of the fall of Satan in this account of the fall of Babylon. Humanity did the same thing. Babylon was just the latest manifestation of Babel (it is the same word in Hebrew). Babel was the ancient city in which humanity came together to build a tower "that reaches to the heavens" (Genesis 11:4). It could be from the S Club 7 songbook! But in judgment God thwarted their plans by sending a multiplicity of languages to confuse and confound them.

And Belshazzar is not the last. 2 Thessalonians 2:4 echoes this language when it speaks of the **antichrist**: "He will oppose and will exalt himself over everything that is called God or is worshipped, so that he sets himself up in God's temple, proclaiming himself to be God". Overreaching power has been embodied in successive idolatrous empires. But each in turn falls. The cycle repeats itself once more—and will do until Christ returns.

The point is this: no matter how far your star rises, no matter how high you climb, in the end "you are brought down … to the depths of the pit" (Isaiah **14:15**). The person whose status you envy will one day hit rock bottom.

We so easily get sucked into thinking human glory and status are what matters. But this is insane. Literally. Nebuchadnezzar became insane when he thought he had made it. Daniel 4 describes a dream which Nebuchadnezzar had and which was interpreted by Daniel. Daniel said that God would judge Nebuchadnezzar for his pride.

He would lose his sanity, live like an animal and be driven away by his people. Despite this warning, what Daniel predicted came to pass. Nebuchadnezzar declared, "Is not this the great Babylon I have built as the royal residence, by my mighty power and for the glory of my majesty?" (Daniel 4:30). That was the real moment of insanity. He only became sane again when "he acknowledged that the Most High God is sovereign over all kingdoms on earth" (Daniel 5:21).

Nebuchadnezzar was extreme in both his pride and his fall. But he represents all of us. In **14:24** Isaiah says:

"The LORD Almighty has sworn,

'Surely, as I have planned, so it will be,

and as I have purposed, so it will happen.'"

This is sanity: believing that God is God and we are human; believing that our lives are not in our own hands but in his hands. Of course we affect the course of our lives. We are not mere puppets with no initiative, agency or responsibility. But can you really control your wealth, your health, your family, your future? Can you eliminate risk? Think about it. Sanity is found as we recognise that God is in control.

Questions for reflection

1. In what regard are you most tempted to seek to "rise"? What do you do to pursue human glory—be that beauty, wealth, popularity or something else?

2. Why is seeking human glory pointless? Why is it dangerous?

3. When you remember that God is control, how does that change the way you live?

PART TWO

Success is turned upside down

In **14:16** people say of the fallen king, "Is this the man who shook the earth and made kingdoms tremble?" As this king advanced into the battle, it felt like the earth was shaking, and people trembled before him. But compare this with what God says in 13:13:

"Therefore I will make the heavens tremble;
and the earth will shake from its place
at the wrath of the LORD Almighty,
in the day of his burning anger."

It is a complete reversal! The king who made kingdoms tremble will tremble before God. The king of Babylon will not even be properly buried (**14:18-21**).

In **14:17** the people continue: "Is this ... the man who made the world a wilderness, who overthrew its cities?" Again, compare this to 13:19-22: "Babylon, the jewel of kingdoms, the pride and glory of the Babylonians, will be overthrown by God ... She will never be inhabited" and "desert creatures will lie there". The king who overthrew nations will be overthrown.

When it defeated Jerusalem in 587 BC, Babylon was the largest city in the world. It was the first city in human history to exceed 200,000 people. Where is it today? It is a ruin in the desert—just as Isaiah said in 13:20.

In 1983 Saddam Hussein started to rebuild the city, portraying himself as a new Nebuchadnezzar. He had his name inscribed on the bricks, just as Nebuchadnezzar used to do. He had a large portrait of himself alongside Nebuchadnezzar put up at the entrance. Signs throughout the city declared, "This was built by Saddam Hussein, son of Nebuchadnezzar, to glorify Iraq". And yet today the city of Babylon is still a ruin in the desert.

The person whose wealth you envy will not take it with them.

"They are not to rise to inherit the land," says **14:21**. There is no inheritance in hell. After delivering this oracle against Babylon, God immediately starts talking about Assyria (**14:25-27**)—probably because Assyria is Judah's immediate threat as Isaiah speaks. The point is that God is sovereign over *all* nations. Even if you make it in this life, we all face death.

Reader's guide

Isaiah 13 - 14

Isaiah 13 – 23 contains prophecies against the nations around Judah that appear to be drawn from across Isaiah's ministry. Chapters 13 – 14 describe the fall of Babylon, the empire to the north that arose after Isaiah's lifetime. Isaiah also prophesies against the Philistines, the old enemy of God's people. "The rod" in 14:29 is probably David and his dynasty. The Philistines should not rejoice in Judah's problems because they, too, will be defeated by the Assyrians (14:31-32).

Isaiah 15 - 16

*Moab was to the south-east of Judah, on the other side of the River Jordan. The Moabites were the descendants of Lot (**Abraham's** nephew) through an incestuous relationship with his daughter (Genesis 19:36-37). Isaiah laments the fall of Moab because of her pride (16:6-7). 16:3-5 is hard to translate, but is probably a plea to Moab to protect refugees from Judah (16:4 could be "O Moab, let the fugitives stay with you"). 16:5 promises that, whatever Moab's decision, a king will come (a promised fulfilled in Jesus) who will provide a refuge for God's people.*

Isaiah 17

Isaiah prophesies against Damascus, the capital of Aram (sometimes known as Syria). Aram was the nation which had ganged up with the northern tribes of Israel against Judah (7:1). So the northern tribes of Israel (or Ephraim) are also included in Aram's judgment (17:3-11).

Isaiah suggests that some within Israel will turn back to God as a result of this judgment (17:7-8).

Isaiah 18 - 20

These chapters contain three prophecies about the Egyptians (Cush is the upper Nile region and therefore linked to Egypt). "There is nothing Egypt can do" when God comes in judgment (19:15). Even their idols tremble before God (19:1). Chapter 20 describes a specific moment when Egypt and Cush would be defeated by the Assyrian Empire. But 18:3 shows that these warnings are a sign for "all you people of the world"; at the end of history God will judge all nations as he once judged the nations around Judah. Yet in the midst of the judgment comes an amazing promise that one day there will be a new exodus, not from Egypt but for Egypt (19:18-25). God will rescue them from their oppressors, make himself known to them and call them "my people"—just as he once did for Israel when the Egyptians were their oppressors.

Isaiah 21

"The Desert by the Sea" is a reference to Babylon (21:9), which would (as Isaiah predicts here) suddenly fall to the Medes and Persians (21:2). 21:9 is echoed in the book of Revelation (18:2). Revelation uses "Babylon" to describe the Roman Empire—another empire which destroyed the temple in Jerusalem but which would eventually fall. It's a reminder that idolatrous powers come and go in history. Isaiah 21 ends with prophecies against Edom and Arabia (21:11-17). Morning, in the literal sense of a new day, may be coming, but night, in the metaphorical sense of judgment, is also coming (21:12).

Isaiah 22

"The Valley of Vision" describes Judah and Jerusalem (22:8-9). It is telling that Judah is included in this list of judgments against **Gentile** nations, for she has failed to be the place of "vision" where God's word is proclaimed. 22:13 is cited by Paul in 1 Corinthians 15:32 as the slogan of the broken morality of those who have no hope of resurrection.

In 22:15-25 Isaiah prophesies against two individuals. Shebna is probably the leading official in King Hezekiah's court mentioned in 37:2. It's a foreign name, which may explain why Isaiah asks, "What are you doing here?" (22:16) For Isaiah Shebna is a symbol of Judah being influenced by unbelievers. He would be replaced by Eliakim (22:20-24), but Eliakim would be unable to prevent Jerusalem's fall (22:25).

Isaiah 23

Tyre was a coastal state to the north of Judah and a great trading nation. Like other nations, she would be brought low because of her pride (23:9). Eventually she would be restored and once again ply her trade. But this time her profits would be dedicated to the LORD (23:17-18; see also 18:7). It is a picture of the way the glory of the nations will be incorporated in God's kingdom—an idea we meet again in Isaiah 60 and Revelation 21:24-26.

In **14:26** Isaiah says, "This is the plan determined for the whole world; this is the hand stretched out over all nations". "The hand stretched out" is a phrase from the exodus. God stretched out his hand in judgment over Egypt. Now Isaiah is promising a new exodus and that new exodus will mean judgment on Babylon. But not just Babylon. Babylon's judgment is a pointer to the judgment of all humanity. This is why **14:29** says, "Do not rejoice, all you Philistines, that the rod that struck you is broken". Why not? Because Philistia will also be judged by God (**14:30**). Then Isaiah addresses all the surrounding nations and beyond in chapters 15 – 23:

- Moab (15:1 – 16:14)
- Damascus—the capital of Aram (17:1-14)
- Cush—the upper Nile region (18:1-7)
- Egypt—the lower Nile region (19:1-17)
- Egypt and Cush together (20:1-6)
- Babylon (again) (21:1-10)

- Edom—symbolically called Dumah or "silence" (21:11-12)

- Arabia (21:13-17)

- Jerusalem—the capital of Judah (22:1-14)

- Tyre (23:1-18)

With the possible exception of the prophecy about Philistia (**14:28-32**), which may have been proclaimed before their envoys (**14:32**), these prophecies were spoken to the people of Judah. They show that in reality all the people they fear are under God's control.

I suspect it is hard to imagine on a sunny day in your town or city as people go about their business or families spend time in the local park that God's judgment will one day fall. But then the Babylonians found it hard to imagine that their glory would ever end. God is inviting us to look across history, see how empires have fallen and realise that these are all pointers to a greater and more terrible day of judgment when we will all give an account before God. We are invited to read the writing on the wall *for us*: Mene, tekel: God has numbered *your* days; *you* have been weighed on the scales, and you have been found wanting.

Refuge and welcome

But there is a refuge from God's judgment. In **14:32** Isaiah says, "The LORD has established Zion, and in her his afflicted people will find refuge". Zion was the hill upon which Jerusalem was built. But Isaiah is not talking about physical Jerusalem because in chapter 22 Jerusalem is included in the nations that will be judged. Isaiah 22:5 says:

"The Lord, the LORD Almighty, has a day
of tumult and trampling and terror
in the Valley of Vision,
a day of battering down walls
and of crying out to the mountains."

Isaiah describes Jerusalem's inhabitants tearing down their houses to build up the wall and yet refusing to look to God (22:10-11). So it is no use running to Jerusalem; Jerusalem will fall like all the other nations.

This is why Isaiah says "Zion" and not "Jerusalem". He is talking about the people of God, the faithful remnant, those who find refuge in Jesus Christ (16:5; 22:20-24). And this is why chapter 14, which is about the fall of Babylon, begins with a focus on the future of God's people:

"The LORD will have compassion on Jacob;
once again he will choose Israel
and will settle them in their own land.
Foreigners will join them
and unite with the descendants of Jacob." (**14:1**)

The people of Judah would be exiled in Babylon, but one day the Babylonian Empire would fall so God's people would come home in victory (**14:2-6**). Babylonian exile was a picture of a larger exile—humanity's exile from God. But now the forces of sin and death which enslave us have been overthrown through the death and resurrection of Christ. And one day God will gather his people and bring us home. Not only will God's people be restored, but the land will be restored in a new creation: "All the lands are at rest and peace; they break into singing" (**14:7-8**).

This vision of restoration and welcome becomes positively audacious and outrageous in 19:19-25. God says he will "strike Egypt with a plague" (19:22). That's not the audacious part! God did that before during the exodus (Exodus 7 – 12). No true Israelite is going to complain about Egypt being on the wrong end of God's judgment. After all, Egypt is the old enemy. But then Isaiah adds, "He will strike them and heal them. They will turn to the LORD, and he will respond to their pleas and heal them" (19:22).

Isaiah says, "When they cry out to the LORD because of their oppressors, he will send them a saviour and defender, and he will rescue them" (19:20). Again, this language is taken from the story of the exodus, when Israel cried out to God because of their oppression in

Egypt (Exodus 2:23-24; 3:7-9). But Isaiah is not talking about Israel; he's talking about Egypt. It's the Egyptians who will cry out to the LORD, and it's to the Egyptians that God will send a saviour. Egypt are going to acknowledge God and worship him with sacrifices (19:21).

"In that day there will be a highway from Egypt to Assyria. The Assyrians will go to Egypt and the Egyptians to Assyria. The Egyptians and Assyrians will worship together. In that day Israel will be the third, along with Egypt and Assyria, a blessing on the earth. The LORD Almighty will bless them, saying, 'Blessed be Egypt my people, Assyria my handiwork, and Israel my inheritance.'" (19:23-25)

Isaiah describes a highway (19:23). A highway carrying God's people home from exile is a common theme in Isaiah. But here it is Egypt and Assyria, Israel's great enemies, who travel on this highway so that they might worship God together. The outrageous climax comes with God blessing Israel, Egypt and Assyria equally (19:25): "Blessed be Egypt my people, Assyria my handiwork, and Israel my inheritance". The language of "my people", "my handiwork", "my inheritance", which previously has always been used to mark out Israel as God's chosen people, is now used to embrace God's enemies. It is hard to imagine how Isaiah could have proclaimed "Egypt my people" or "Assyria my handiwork" without being arrested for **sedition**. Yet this is God's grace. Eight centuries later Jesus would eat with tax collectors. Tax collectors were seen by their fellow Jews as collaborators with the occupying Roman army. They were the enemies of God, and yet these are the very people whom God's King welcomes. Isaiah presents us with a radical vision that embraces all nations and in which God calls his enemies "my people". Today God is still bringing into his kingdom people who were once his enemies (Colossians 1:21-22)—including many whom we might not have predicted.

> Isaiah presents us with a radical vision: God calls his enemies "my people".

Eternal glory

People are literally hell-bent on "reaching for the stars". And yet human glory, status and success are all so temporary. But you do not need Isaiah to tell you this. You just need to go to any rubbish tip or graveyard. There you will see the future of the stuff you covet and the glory you crave.

As we stand in the rubbish tip and the graveyard, seeing all human glory rotting away, listen to God's words. This is what Paul says in 2 Corinthians 3 – 4: "We all, who ... contemplate the Lord's glory, are being transformed into his image with ever-increasing glory, which comes from the Lord, who is the Spirit" (3:18). Here is a glory that does not rot away or tumble down. This is *ever-increasing* glory. It does not get less and less like human beauty, status or wealth. It grows more and more throughout our lives.

And here is a glory that we do not have to earn or create or build. It is the glory of God, and he shares it with us. All we need to do is *look*! We simply contemplate God's glory, and, as we contemplate it, we are glorified. So where do we look? God's word continues: "For God, who said, 'Let light shine out of darkness,' made his light shine in our hearts to give us the light of the knowledge of God's glory displayed in the face of Christ" (2 Corinthians 4:6). We look into the face of Christ. That is where you will see the glory of God, and that is the look that will transform you.

So it all depends on where you look. Look at the adverts, the glossy magazines, the car on your neighbour's drive and your heart will be pulled towards human glory. But look at God's glory in the face of Christ and your heart will be transformed with ever-increasing glory.

But there is more. 2 Corinthians 4:17 continues: "For our light and momentary troubles are achieving for us an eternal glory that far outweighs them all."

■ Look at the rubbish tip and the graveyard, and what do you see? Human glory is temporary and fleeting.

■ Look at the face of Christ and what do you see? The promise of eternal glory.

■ Look at your troubles in the light of Christ and what do you see? God easing our hearts out of the rubbish tip and showing us to eternal glory.

A friend of mine regularly used to walk by the River Thames in London. On his walk he used to say hello to an elderly gentleman tending his garden in one of the big houses by the river. Then, for several months, my friend did not see this man in his garden. When at last he saw him again, he remarked on his absence. The man explained that his wife had been ill and had died. They had been married for over 60 years. The gentleman said to my friend, "Do you know who I am?" In the area there was a chain of garden centres called Squires. He said, "I'm Mr Squires". He was worth £4 million. But then he said, "I'm 93, and soon I will be gone, and what will it be worth to me then?" My friend told me he walked away thinking, "I'm far richer than Mr Squires."

Questions for reflection

1. Do people you know think much about the fact that they will one day die? What difference do you think it would make to them if they thought about that more?

2. Who do you find it hard to believe could ever be brought into God's kingdom? Do you need to alter the way you speak or act towards them?

3. How can you spend more time "contemplat[ing] the Lord's glory"?

5. GOD JUDGES THE EARTH

FOCUS: ISAIAH 25

The Bible says that one day God will judge humanity. We will all have to stand before him and give an account. Jesus will separate humanity into "sheep" and "goats" for heaven and hell, for life and death (Matthew 25:31-33). It is a truth we perhaps hesitate to mention. We feel happier talking about God's love. We assume talk of hellfire will put people off our message.

Perhaps. But it is also the case that the world is full of reasons for divine judgment. Spend a few minutes scanning a newspaper or watching the television news and you will have a strong sense that something should be done. The human heart has an instinctive longing for justice. We want evil to be punished and wrongs to be righted.

Universal judgment

As we have seen, Isaiah 13 – 23 contains a collection of the prophet's declarations of judgment against the nations around God's people: Babylon, Assyria, Philistia, Moab, Aram, Cush and Egypt, Edom, Arabia and Tyre. Now in chapters 24 – 27 Isaiah's vision of God's coming judgment expands to embrace the devastation of the whole earth. The judgments taking place in history, described in chapters 13 – 23, are pointers to a global judgment at the end of history. The tone is set in the opening of this section:

"See, the LORD is going to lay waste the earth
> and devastate it;
he will ruin its face
> and scatter its inhabitants." (24:1)

The judgments of chapters 13 – 23 are all localised. They speak of nations being defeated and empires collapsing. But the coming day of judgment will be universal. It affects everyone:

"It will be the same
> for priest as for people,
> for the master as for his servant,
> for the mistress as for her servant,
> for seller as for buyer,
> for borrower as for lender,
> for debtor as for creditor." (24:2)

All the distinctions that so often matter in human interactions—between **clergy** and **laity**, between employers and employees, between the haves and the have-nots—will be swept away on that day (24:21-23). The honour and wealth to which people devote so much of their energies will seem meaningless. Think of 24:2 as two columns, and think of the time you devote to moving from one column to the other. On that day such things will count for nothing.

Not only will this judgment affect *everyone*; it will also affect *everything*. "The earth will be *completely* laid waste and *totally* plundered" (24:3, emphasis added). Creation itself will be affected by God's judgment (24:1, 3, 4, 5, 6, 13, 19, 20; 26:21). "A curse consumes the earth," says 24:6. The very fabric of the natural world is affected: "The earth is broken up, the earth is split asunder, the earth is violently shaken" (24:18-19). With the land in such disarray, there will be no resources for celebration (24:7-12). So on that day the message will be: *The party's over!*

"The joyful tambourines are stilled,
> the noise of the revellers has stopped …
No longer do they drink wine with a song;

the beer is bitter to its drinkers …
all joy turns to gloom,
all joyful sounds are banished from the earth." (24:8-9, 11)

Universal sin

God's judgment is relentless: "Whoever flees at the sound of terror will fall into a pit; whoever climbs out of the pit will be caught in a snare" (24:18). If you find this vision disturbing, that's because it is meant to shake us from our complacency. The violence of God is terrible to behold. But God's judgment is not arbitrary or indiscriminate. His judgment is the reaction of his holiness to our sin. It's the response of his love to the suffering we inflict on one another. In 24:5 Isaiah says:

"The earth is defiled by its people;
   they have disobeyed the laws,
violated the statutes
   and broken the everlasting covenant."

God had made a covenant with his people Israel at Mount Sinai, which they had broken. But what about us, those of us who are Gentiles? We were not part of that covenant. But Isaiah takes us back to an older covenant: a covenant as old as time. The act of creation implies a covenant in which the creature is bound to honour and obey the Creator (Romans 2:14-15). And this covenant has been broken by all humanity. The reason for universal judgment is universal sin.

As a result, the earth itself is defiled and cursed. "Therefore a curse consumes the earth; its people must bear their guilt." (Isaiah 24:6; Genesis 3:17-20). It is as if the blood of human violence has drained into the soil and the earth bears it like a scar. The dead have been buried in the ground, but they cry out from the grave—like the blood of **Abel** crying out for justice (Genesis 4:10). And so one day the earth is going to turn on us:

"See, the LORD is coming out of his dwelling
   to punish the people of the earth for their sins.

The earth will disclose the blood shed on it;
the earth will conceal its slain no longer." (Isaiah 26:21)

Creation already endures God's curse. When Adam first sinned, God placed the earth under a curse (Genesis 3:17-19). Paul speaks of creation groaning as it waits for its liberation from this curse (Romans 8:19-22). The land of Israel was supposed to be a picture of this liberation—a land flowing with milk and honey as its enjoyed God's blessing instead of enduring God's curse. But Israel's sin meant the land would be devastated and depopulated. This is what happened when the Babylonians invaded and the people were exiled. But it points forward to the final judgment. 2 Peter 3:10 says: "The day of the Lord will come like a thief. The heavens will disappear with a roar; the elements will be destroyed by fire, and the earth and everything done in it will be laid bare." But this is not the end of the story for God's creation. God is not going to throw this earth into the garbage bin. Instead he is going to purge it and then renew it. A few verses later, 2 Peter 3:13 says: "In keeping with his promise we are looking forward to a new heaven and a new earth, where righteousness dwells."

Reader's guide

Isaiah 24

Isaiah 13 – 23 described specific judgment on specific nations. Chapter 24 scales this up to describe universal judgment, which extends even to the land. This chapter highlights the way that judgments in history are pointers to the final judgment at the end of time.

Isaiah 25

*At the end of history God will **vindicate** his people, and they will enjoy a feast forever in God's presence without the threat of death.*

Isaiah 26

Isaiah 26 celebrates the refuge that God provides (26:1-6), but it also expresses a longing for God to come to vindicate his reputation

(26:7-11). Isaiah acknowledges that God alone can save (26:12-19). The chapter ends with an allusion to the Passover night described in Exodus 12, as God's people find refuge in their homes while God comes in judgment (Isaiah 26:20-21), just as the Israelites found refuge with the blood of the Passover lamb daubed over their doorframes (Exodus 12). It's a picture of finding refuge in Christ, our Passover Lamb.

Isaiah 27

Isaiah 27 begins with the defeat of Leviathan, a monster who symbolises the forces of chaos (27:1). In 5:1-7 Isaiah described God's people as a fruitless vineyard. Now he describes the renewal of this vineyard (27:2-6). It points to Jesus, the true Vine, through whom we can bear fruit (John 15:1-8). Isaiah 27:7-11 describes God's judgment against Judah, but the chapter ends with God gathering his people back to his holy mountain (27:12-13). These verses are being fulfilled through the mission of the church as God gathers his chosen people into the church.

How should we respond when the Lord comes out to punish the people of the earth? The declarations of devastation in chapters 24 – 27 are interwoven with songs (24:14-16; **25:1-12**; 26:1-18). These songs provide a proper orientation to what God is going to do.

Praise God for the great reversal

Isaiah 25 is one of these songs. It's in five sections with the first and last sections parallelling one another, the second and penultimate sections parallelling one another, and a core central section, which is the heart of its message. So **25:1-3** and **10-12** pick up the same themes. They begin:

"Lord, you are my God;
    I will exalt you and praise your name,
  for in perfect faithfulness

you have done wonderful things,
> things planned long ago.
You have made the city a heap of rubble,
> the fortified town a ruin,
the foreigners' stronghold a city no more;
> it will never be rebuilt." (**25:1-2**)

Isaiah describes a great reversal: the strong become weak; the weak become strong. The ruthless will be subdued (**25:3**). The same theme is reprised at the end of the song. God's hand will be on his people—represented by "this mountain". Meanwhile the land of Moab (Israel's ancient enemy) will be trampled like straw into manure (**25:10**).

Notice the "up" and "down" language. God is going to "bring down their pride" (**25:11**). Their *high* thoughts of themselves will come crashing *down*. He's going to "bring *down*" their "*high* fortified walls and lay them *low*" (**25:12**, emphasis added). Up is going to be down, and down is going to be up. Isaiah uses the same imagery in 26:5-6:

"He humbles those who dwell on high,
> he lays the lofty city low;
he levels it to the ground
> and casts it down to the dust.
Feet trample it down—
> the feet of the oppressed,
> the footsteps of the poor."

It is a theme Jesus himself echoes: "All those who exalt themselves will be humbled, and those who humble themselves will be exalted" (Luke 14:11).

Isaiah has a powerful image for the impact of God's judgment in **25:11**. He says it will be like when "swimmers stretch out their hands to swim". That makes perfect sense when you are pulling yourself through the water. But take the water away and you are left with people clawing desperately at empty air. There is nothing to take hold of as people are dragged down to the dust from which they came (**25:11-12**; Genesis 2:7; 3:14, 19).

This is a song of praise to God. But why are we praising him? Because he has made the city a heap of rubble. In the original Hebrew language in which these words were written, Isaiah **25:2** begins with the word "for", so **25:2** is the reason for the praise of **25:1**. The language of **25:2** echoes 24:10: "The ruined city lies desolate". God warns of his coming judgment in chapter 24, and *therefore* his people sing his praise in chapter 25.

Perhaps this feels counterintuitive to us. Why will we sing when we see destruction? But let me suggest that in fact it is deeply intuitive and deeply instinctive. How many hundreds of movies have you seen in which at the climax the bad guy gets his comeuppance and your heart exults? Now look across human history and across our world. See the depth of human evil and the pain it has caused. A day is coming when God will bring all of this to an end. God will declare, "Enough". At last justice will be done. The

> A day is coming when God will declare, "Enough".

evil that so often flourishes in our world will flourish no more. Those people with the wealth and power to escape justice will escape justice no more. Wrongs will be righted. Our hearts will exult; they will exalt our God (**25:1**). In 26:9 Isaiah says, "My soul yearns for you," but what he yearns for in this context is God's justice.

The phrase "perfect faithfulness" in **25:1** translates two words with the same root. So it literally means something like "faithfulness and more faithfulness" or "faithfully faithful". God speaks again and again in the Bible of this coming day of judgment—of a great reversal—and he will prove faithfully faithful to his word.

Isaiah is talking about a day in the future. "God will bring down their pride," says **25:11**. It has not happened yet. But we anticipate that day in our praise. Consider again **25:1**: "LORD, you are my God; I will exalt you and praise your name". Notice the "up" and "down" language again. "I will exalt you" is literally "I will lift you up". Of course, we don't add to God's majesty or honour. Instead, Isaiah is saying, *I will recognise and praise your exalted status.* After all, when he saw God in the temple, what did he see? "I saw the Lord, high and exalted" (6:1).

On earth people ignore and despise God. "LORD, your hand is lifted high," says 26:11, "but they do not see it". God is down at the bottom of their list of priorities. Instead, they look up to the rich, the celebrities, the powerful. But we Christians will exalt our God. He's the one we will look up to, and his glory is our top priority. Even the great superpowers of Isaiah's day, Egypt and Assyria, will one day worship the LORD (27:12-13).

When we look at the way evil people seem to do so well in life, we can feel disoriented. That was the psalmist's experience:

"Surely God is good to Israel,
　　to those who are pure in heart.
But as for me, my feet had almost slipped;
　　I had nearly lost my foothold.
For I envied the arrogant
　　when I saw the prosperity of the wicked." (Psalm 73:1-3)

The moral order that we expect in the universe does not always seem to be there. We wonder whether God can be trusted or whether we have made the right choice to pursue godliness. But the coming of God's judgment reorients us towards God and his ways. It enables us to look beyond the present moment and see the bigger perspective. We weigh things in the light of eternity and find our present troubles to be "light and momentary" (2 Corinthians 4:17). Isaiah says the day is coming when the glory of other lords will fade from memory and only the glory of God will remain (26:12-15). So it is that Isaiah says:

"The path of the righteous is level;
　　you, the Upright One, make the way of the righteous smooth.
Yes, LORD, walking in the way of your laws,
　　we wait for you;

your name and renown
    are the desire of our hearts." (26:7-8)

Isaiah is not promising that everything will work out the way we would like it. This is not a promise of health and wealth. It is a promise that seeing the world from the perspective of eternity will keep our footing secure as we walk in the ways of the LORD.

Questions for reflection

1. How does Isaiah 24 inform your view of creation?

2. Why is God's judgment a good thing? How would you explain this to someone who thinks it isn't?

3. What overall impression of God do you get in the passages discussed above?

PART TWO

Isaiah warns of universal judgment. But he calls on God's people to sing. We are to praise God for the great reversal that is coming. But the songs that Isaiah teaches us to sing also invite us to find refuge from God in God.

Trust God to be our refuge

The next matching pair of sections in chapter 25 is **25:4-5** and **25:9**:

> "You have been a refuge for the poor,
>   a refuge for the needy in their distress,
>   a shelter from the storm
>   and a shade from the heat.
>   For the breath of the ruthless
>   is like a storm driving against a wall
>   and like the heat of the desert.
>   You silence the uproar of foreigners;
>   as heat is reduced by the shadow of a cloud,
>   so the song of the ruthless is stilled." (**25:4-5**)

Isaiah imagines a desert storm with sand blown into our faces. Those who know little of desert life should perhaps imagine instead the violence of a hailstorm. In the midst of the storm, if you step inside and close the door, then all is calm. Perhaps today you feel like your life is in chaos. Or maybe you're caught up in conflict, so much so that you feel as if you're walking in the middle of a storm. Isaiah invites us to step into God—to make him our refuge and feel the calm his care brings.

Or Isaiah hears the clamour of a foreign army: the snorting of their horses, the sound of sword on shield, the violence of the battle songs. Perhaps today your head is filled with noise—with accusations, threats, scorn, arguments. Isaiah invites us to find shelter in God. It's as if you step inside and all the noise outside becomes muffled. "The song of the ruthless," says Isaiah, "is stilled" (**25:5**).

Or Isaiah likens the trials of life to the heat of the sun. Sometimes we say, "The heat is on" when pressures build up. Think of how we wilt in the heat. You can put more clothes on if you're cold, but there's a limit to what you can take off when it's hot! There's no escape from the heat. But God, Isaiah says, is "a shade from the heat" (**25:4**). God is like a cloud, and Isaiah invites us to live in the shade of that cloud.

In the context of chapter 25 Isaiah's point is that God is consistent—he is "faithfully faithful". It's not that God sometimes sides with the powerful and sometimes with the powerless. It's not that God sometimes lets people get away with evil and sometimes he doesn't. He's not whimsical or arbitrary.

God's interventions in history to judge—bringing down nations as described in Isaiah 13 – 23—are a pointer to the way he will act on the final day of judgment. And God's interventions in history to save his people—to shelter and shade them—are a pointer to the way he will act on the final day to save his people. The reason that God does not yet act to end evil is because he is giving people an opportunity to repent. The delay is not a sign of inconsistency; it's a sign of his patience and mercy (Romans 2:4-5; 2 Peter 3:9).

How should we respond to the coming of God's judgment? One answer is to stay at home with the doors locked! In 26:20 Isaiah gives this advice:

"Go, my people, enter your rooms
and shut the doors behind you;
hide yourselves for a little while
until his wrath has passed by."

Of course it's crazy to think we can escape God's judgment simply by hiding behind the sofa. But there was a time when God's people really did escape his judgment by staying at home. On the night of Passover, when God moved in judgment through the land of Egypt, Israel were spared by staying at home. But it wasn't the structural integrity of their houses that saved them, but the blood of the Passover lamb daubed around the lintels. The Passover lamb was a picture of Jesus, the Lamb of God, who takes away the sin of the world. We can face God's judgment with confidence only by hiding beneath the blood of Christ. We find refuge from God in God.

In chapter 26 Isaiah changes the imagery. Instead of a safe house, we have a safe city (26:1-2). But again, it is not so much a safe city as a safe God in whom we trust. Isaiah continues:

"You will keep in perfect peace
those whose minds are steadfast,
because they trust in you.
Trust in the LORD for ever,
for the LORD, the LORD himself, is the Rock eternal." (26:3-4)

The "LORD himself" is our refuge. The twin realities of human sin and divine judgment give us powerful cause to be afraid. But those who trust in Christ can face the future with "perfect peace". This is the secret of true assurance. It can be helpful to look at the changes God has produced in our lives through the work of the Spirit. These can function as powerful confirmations that we are born again. But ultimately true assurance is found not in looking at ourselves but in looking to Christ. He, and he alone, is the source of perfect peace.

In the meantime, the storm may rage, and the heat may beat down on us. But we can entrust ourselves to God, confident that a new day is coming. Isaiah reprises this theme in **25:9**:

"In that day they will say,
'Surely this is our God;
we trusted in him, and he saved us.
This is the LORD, we trusted in him;
let us rejoice and be glad in his salvation.'"

At the end of time, God's people will say, "This is our God". He is "faithfully faithful". "We trusted in him", and it was worth it, for "he saved us". He sheltered us through the storm; he shaded us from the heat.

The word "trust" in **25:9** is literally "wait". It is a declaration that we waited for God—not impatiently with our fingers drumming on the table but patiently in trust:

"Surely this is our God;
> we waited for him, and he saved us.
This is the LORD, we waited for him;
> let us rejoice and be glad in his salvation."

One day we will say, "We felt the heat, we lived through the storm and we waited for God. The heat grew hotter, and still we waited for our God. The storm raged on, but still we waited for our God. We waited for him, but we did not wait for ever, nor did we wait in vain. The storm has passed, and a new creation has dawned. Let us rejoice and be glad in his salvation."

Look forward to victory

The central section of this song is **25:6-8**, which begins by depicting an amazing feast:

"On this mountain the LORD Almighty will prepare
> a feast of rich food for all peoples,
a banquet of aged wine—
> the best of meats and the finest of wines. (**25:6**)

Isaiah is describing your future if you're in Christ by faith, and it is a feast. "A feast of rich foods" is literally "a feast of fatness", and "the best of meats" uses the same "fatty" word again. We get the same repetition and intensification with the wine: "aged wine" becomes "refined aged wine"—something like port, presumably. So the sentence is literally something like, "a feast of fatty food and aged wine with fatty meat and refined aged wine". No one is worrying about their cholesterol! Three times chapter 24 says God's judgment on the earth means it produces no wine (24:7, 9, 11), and so the songs of the revellers will be silenced (24:8). But not among God's people. "On this mountain" the wine flows, and songs are sung.

A feast speaks of satisfaction. Our emptiness will be filled; our thirst will be quenched; our needs will be met. But a feast also speaks of communion. To be invited to a meal is a sign of friendship. Here God invites us to a meal (see also 55:1-2). It's a sign that our relationship with him has been restored. We will live for ever in communion with the triune God, sharing the joy of the Father and Son through the Spirit.

But it's not just fatty food that's on the menu. Death itself is going to be swallowed up.

"On this mountain he will destroy
    the shroud that enfolds all peoples,
the sheet that covers all nations;
    he will swallow up death for ever.
The Sovereign LORD will wipe away the tears
    from all faces;
he will remove his people's disgrace
    from all the earth.
The LORD has spoken." (**25:7-8**)

A shroud is the cloth with which you cover a dead body. Isaiah says all the nations are covered with a death shroud. Even as we live, death haunts us. It has us in its folds. But God is going to destroy death. Through the resurrection of Jesus, says Paul (echoing Isaiah **25:8**), "death has been swallowed up in victory" (1 Corinthians 15:54). In the present "the earth is defiled" (24:5), but on that day God will remove our disgrace (**25:8**; 27:7-9).

> Death has us in its folds. But God is going to destroy death.

At the moment, the earth sucks in the dead as we return to the dust (**25:12**). People today place great hope in the power of modern medicine to cure, even though ultimately modern medicine has a 100 per cent failure rate. It cures many illnesses, but every patient dies in the end. People invest huge amounts of energy—quite literally—in working out and staying fit, all in the vain hope of remaining young. But Isaiah exposes the futility of these false hopes. He pictures humanity as a pregnant woman writhing in labour as it attempts to create a future for itself. But in the end we only give birth to wind (26:17-18). Think of people puffing and panting in the gym for a perfect body—a body which will one day be eaten by worms. Our attempts to secure our future evaporate before our eyes. I meet many people in my neighbourhood who have worked hard to create a comfortable retirement only to see their hopes crumble as they succumb to ill-health and old age. Isaiah's conclusion on all this effort is powerful and poignant: "We have not brought salvation to the earth, and the people of the world have not come to life" (26:18).

But the salvation Christ has brought to the earth is so different. Isaiah continues:

"But your dead will live, LORD;
    their bodies will rise—
let those who dwell in the dust
    wake up and shout for joy—
your dew is like the dew of the morning;
    the earth will give birth to her dead." (26:19)

When we bury someone, we commit their body to the grave: "Earth to earth, ashes to ashes, dust to dust". But one day "those who dwell in the dust" will "wake up and shout for joy", and "the earth will give birth to her dead" (26:19).

The true vine and the fruitful vineyard

Isaiah extends this promise of restoration in chapter 27. Back in Isaiah 5 the prophet sang a love song using the imagery of a vineyard. He sang of how God nurtured his vineyard.

"He dug it up and cleared it of stones
    and planted it with the choicest vines.
He built a watchtower in it
    and cut out a winepress as well." (5:2)

But when God went to inspect the crop, he found only bad fruit. So he decided to abandon his vineyard and let it become a wasteland. It is a picture of the way in which he chose Israel to be his people, rescued them from slavery, revealed his glory to them at Mount Sinai and planted them in the promised land. Everything was put in place for them to serve him in love. But instead of doing good works, Israel produced only the bad fruit of evil acts. So the tone of the song becomes plaintive:

"What more could have been done for my vineyard
    than I have done for it?
When I looked for good grapes,
    why did it yield only bad?" (5:4)

In chapter 27 God again sings about his vineyard. "In that day" he will restore his people. Again he will watch over his vineyard, water it and guard it (27:2-3). He will confront any weeds like an army marching into battle (27:4-5). As a result:

"In days to come Jacob will take root,
    Israel will bud and blossom
    and fill all the world with fruit." (27:6)

This is the background to the declaration by Jesus: "I am the true vine" (John 15:1). Humanity has failed to produce the fruit of good works. Only Jesus has produced a true harvest of righteousness. But there is hope for us, and it is found in Christ. We can be fruitful by remaining in him. "I am the vine," Jesus says in John 15:5; "you are the branches. If you remain in me and I in you, you will bear much fruit; apart from me you can do nothing." Jesus again alludes to Isaiah's vineyard in Mark 11:12-25 and 12:1-12, which together suggest that God's beloved vineyard will no longer be associated with the temple and will become instead the community of Jesus, the true Vine.

Questions for reflection

1. How do you tend to respond to the thought of God's judgment? Does this passage challenge you?

2. What does it mean, practically speaking, to "wait for the Lord"?

3. What good fruit do you long to see in your life or the lives of those you know? How does the image of the vine and vineyard encourage you?

6. GOD OFFERS US REST

FOCUS: ISAIAH 28

Has it ever felt like God has gone AWOL—absent without leave? You know what you want God to be doing, but he's not doing it. You know what he ought to be doing, but that's not what he's doing. You're asking him to act, but there's no action. Have you thought that what God is doing in your life is *strange*? Of course you have. It happens all the time. We think we know what God ought to do. But sometimes he surprises us and perhaps disappoints us. We don't like it. *This is not the way I would do it.*

Isaiah 28 – 33 contains a series of "sermons", all of which begin with the word "Woe" or, more literally, an attention-grabbing declaration akin to "Hey" (**28:1**; 29:1, 15; 30:1; 31:1; 33:1). Back in chapters 7 – 8, Isaiah had invited King Ahaz, the king of Judah, to trust in God in the face of military threat from Aram and the northern tribes of Israel. But Ahaz chose instead to form an alliance with Assyria. For a while that had looked like a good option as Assyria defeated Judah's enemies. But Assyria the saviour soon became Assyria the tyrant. So now it's Assyria that's the threat, and Assyria is the regional superpower. Judah (now under King Hezekiah) has jumped out of the frying pan and into the mother of all fires.

Some in Judah want to make a deal with Egypt to secure help against Assyria. This might look like the obvious political move. But Isaiah predicts that the outcome will be the same as it was when they looked to Assyria for help. He calls it "a covenant with death" (**28:15**, **18**).

"Woe to the obstinate children ... forming an alliance, but not by my Spirit" (30:1). For help, they look to Egypt, "whose help is utterly useless" (30:7; 31:1-9). They are seeking refuge in lies (**28:15**; 30:2-3). "The Egyptians are mere mortals and not God" (31:3).

What God's people want him to do is to defeat the Assyrians. But God doesn't appear to be in the picture. I wonder what you want God to do that he's not doing. Is God AWOL? Isaiah's message is that God is at work, but he may sometimes be at work in strange ways.

The futility of human strength

Isaiah 28 contains the first in this series of "woe sermons". It begins with Isaiah talking about two "wreaths" or crowns (**28:1**, **3**, **5**). His message begins, "Woe to that wreath, the pride of Ephraim's drunkards". "Ephraim" is another name for the northern kingdom of Israel. Twice Isaiah describes "his glorious beauty, set on the head of a fertile valley" (**28:1**, **4**). It's like a scene from a picture postcard. But it's about to be ruined. God is about to send the Assyrian army to rip through it like a hailstorm (**28:2**). The people of Israel are about to be plucked from their homes like ripe figs being plucked from a tree (**28:4**). The media love to show before-and-after photographs when hurricanes and floods have taken place. That's what Isaiah is doing in these verses. Israel is full of national pride and self-confidence. But it's misplaced. It's flimsy. They're sitting in a garden shed as the hurricane descends and the floods arise. They trust in their own strength. But they will not stand.

In **28:5-6** Isaiah speaks of another "wreath":

"In that day the LORD Almighty
    will be a glorious crown,
a beautiful wreath
    for the remnant of his people.
He will be ... a source of strength
    to those who turn back the battle at the gate."

Israel think they can withstand the onslaught of Assyria, but they are wrong (30:15-17). Only those who trust in God can stand in the midst of the battle (**28:6**). Isaiah exposes the futility of human strength. True strength is found with God.

The futility of human wisdom

In **28:9-10** Isaiah describes the reaction to his ministry:

"Who is it he is trying to teach?
    To whom is he explaining his message?
To children weaned from their milk,
    to those just taken from the breast?
For it is:
    do this, do that,
    a rule for this, a rule for that;
    a little here, a little there."

28:10 appears to be the equivalent of "Blah, blah, blah". Isaiah is quoting the people. This is what they say when Isaiah speaks: *Who's he talking to? This is just for children. On and on he goes. Blah, blah, blah.* "Whatever!" we might say today.

Instead the people prefer the visions of drunken prophets (**28:7-8**). Whether their drunkenness is literal or symbolic (as 29:9-12 suggests) doesn't really matter. The point is that they don't see clearly. But this is what people prefer because they don't want to be confronted with God. People don't want to listen to God's word. They've closed their eyes and put their fingers in their ears. They prefer manmade rules to God's offer of salvation (29:13-14; see Mark 7:6-7 and 1 Corinthians 1:19). In Isaiah 30:10-11 the people say:

"Give us no more visions of what is right!
Tell us pleasant things,
    prophesy illusions ...
and stop confronting us
    with the Holy One of Israel!"

Christians tell the world, "Jesus is the only way." "We are responsible for our behaviour." "We must give an account to God." "Those outside of Christ will be eternally judged." And what do people say? "Tell us pleasant things; prophesy illusions." It's about as logical as standing on the Titanic saying, "Don't tell me the ship is sinking because drowning is such an unpleasant subject." Isaiah says it's like seeing a collapsing wall and taking refuge beneath it (30:12-14; **28:13**).

A couple of years ago a friend started coming to church. He loved it. He loved the singing. He loved the preaching. He found it all very "inspiring". Until, that is, we spoke of sin and repentance. Sin and repentance are not "inspiring"! They don't make you feel good about yourself. In effect, my friend's response was, "Tell me pleasant things and stop confronting me with the Holy One of Israel!"

> They shout "Blah, blah, blah", and wonder why they don't hear God's voice.

We close our eyes and put our fingers in our ears. And then we complain that God doesn't speak to us! People literally walk down the road with earbuds in. They put the radio on in the car. They spend their free time on social media. And then they complain that they can't hear God! They do everything they can to distract themselves—to remove any moments of reflection—and then complain that God is elusive. They drown him out, shouting, "Blah, blah, blah", and wonder why they don't hear his voice.

We Christians can do this. We can be busy, busy, busy with ministry, and then wonder why we can't hear God's voice or don't feel his presence. I don't mean hearing words or voices. I mean hearing God speaking personally to us through his word. Sometimes we can drown him out with our all activity.

"Stop confronting us with the Holy One of Israel," the people say in 30:11. But "the Holy One of Israel" is who God is. This is one of Isaiah's favourite ways of referring to God, and it stems from his encounter with God in chapter 6, where he heard the seraphim crying, "Holy, holy, holy". So God responds:

"Very well then, with foreign lips and strange tongues
    God will speak to this people,
to whom he said,
    'This is the resting-place, let the weary rest';
and, 'This is the place of repose'—
    but they would not listen.
So then, the word of the LORD to them will become:
    [blah, blah, blah]—
so that as they go they will fall backwards;
    they will be injured and snared and captured."

(Adapted from **28:11-13**)

If the people say God's words are "blah, blah, blah", then "blah, blah, blah" is what they will hear: the foreign words of a foreign army. The language spoken on the streets of their towns will be Assyrian, and it will be coming from the lips of an invading army. *How's your Assyrian?* Isaiah is saying, in effect. *Because that's what you're going to be hearing.*

Two audiences

So far Isaiah has appeared to be speaking to the northern kingdom of Israel. He begins, "Woe to that wreath, the pride of Ephraim's drunkards"—"Ephraim" is another term for Israel (**28:1**). But **28:14** says, "Therefore hear the word of the LORD, you scoffers who rule this people in Jerusalem". Jerusalem was the capital of the southern kingdom of Judah. It turns out that really this sermon is a message for Judah. Isaiah is saying, *Look at what's happened to Israel, and learn the lesson.* They trusted in their own strength and in their own wisdom, and they ended up being wiped out by Assyria.

This is Isaiah's message because at the moment Judah is not learning the lessons of Israel's history. They sought help from Assyria when threatened by Aram and the northern tribes of Israel (Isaiah 7 – 8), but Assyria soon became the threat. Now they are seeking help from another superpower, Egypt, to combat the threat of Assyria. Chapter 30 describes how the people of Judah have sent envoys to Pharaoh to make an alliance. "They have officials in Zoan and their envoys have arrived in Hanes", it says in 30:4. Isaiah 30:6 says, "Through a land of hardship and distress, of lions and lionesses, of adders and darting snakes, the envoys carry their riches on donkeys' backs, their treasures on the humps of camels, to that unprofitable nation". They're on a risky journey through dangerous territory to buy the help of Egypt. But Isaiah says it will be "unprofitable". They will not get a return on their investment. Egypt's help will be "utterly useless" (30:7).

Their solution is an alliance with a superpower—even though this is how they got into this problem in the first place! Have they learnt nothing? This is Assyria all over again. King Ahaz made a deal with a superpower which came back to bite him. And Judah's solution to the resulting problem is another deal with every prospect of the same outcome. It's sometimes said that the definition of insanity is to keep doing the same thing over and over again, each time expecting a different result!

But not only is this Assyria all over again (in other words, repeating the mistake made by King Ahaz); this is Egypt all over again. Egypt is the new Egypt! One of the big themes of Isaiah is the promise of a new exodus (30:27-33; 31:5, 8). Just as God rescued his people from slavery in Egypt under Moses, so he will again lead them out of exile. But what do they do? They offer themselves as slaves to Egypt—as a **vassal state**! God promises to repeat the exodus; they put it into reverse.

In chapter 28 Isaiah mocks their claims. The quote in **28:15** is not literally what the people were saying; it's Isaiah's parody of their claims. *We have entered into a covenant with Egypt,* they proclaim. *More like a covenant with death,* says Isaiah. *We have made Pharaoh our refuge,* they proclaim. In effect Isaiah says, *What you really mean is "We have made a lie our refuge".*

Verse 15 continues, "We have made a lie our refuge and falsehood our hiding-place". This is our culture. Confronted with their sin, confronted with God's judgment, confronted with their inadequacies, people take refuge in a lie. "We are basically good." "It's just the way I am." "It's in our DNA." But Christians do this too. What the heart desires, the mind justifies. We find excuses for our sin. We minimise it. We pretend it's inevitable. We blame our circumstances, or redefine sin. We talk about personality types or cultural differences. We talk about Christian freedom. We talk about being contemporary. We take refuge in a lie.

But it doesn't stand up. **28:17-18** picks up the language of **28:15**. In **28:15** the people say:

"We have made a lie our refuge
and falsehood our hiding-place."

But in **28:17** Isaiah says:

"Hail will sweep away your refuge, the lie,
and water will overflow your hiding-place."

In **28:15** the people say:

"We have entered into a covenant with death, with the realm of
the dead we have made an agreement."

But in **28:18** Isaiah says:

"Your covenant with death will be annulled;
your agreement with the realm of the dead will not stand."

In **28:15** the people say:

"When an overwhelming **scourge** sweeps by,
it cannot touch us."

But in **28:18** Isaiah says:

"When the overwhelming scourge sweeps by,
you will be beaten down by it."

Judah's false hopes of being protected from Assyria by Egypt would be swept away, and it was God himself who would do this. "Your covenant with death will be annulled," says Isaiah (**28:15-18**; 33:7-9).

Questions for reflection

1. When have you experienced God working in your life in a strange or unexpected way?

2. What would you say to someone who seems to be shutting their ears to God—either a believer or an unbeliever?

3. What are you tempted to rely on other than God?

PART TWO

We need to remember that there are two original audiences for Isaiah's words. The first audience is the northern kingdom of Israel. The northern kingdom have rejected God; they have been defeated by the Assyrians and wiped from the face of history. They represent humanity apart from Christ. They are a warning of God's judgment. God says, "I will make justice the measuring line and righteousness the **plumb-line**" (**28:17**). When we are measured by God's standard, all of us are found wanting. All of us are condemned. Our only hope is Christ.

Just as Judah should have learnt from the story of Israel, so we should learn from both their stories. In chapters 34 – 35, Isaiah looks beyond the then-current crisis. As in chapters 24 – 27, God's judgment in history becomes a pointer to his coming judgment against all humanity. The LORD "will totally destroy" the nations (34:1-2, 5; see also 30:27-33; 33:1-4, 10-12), and "the stars in the sky will be dissolved" (34:3-4) in a sacrificial offering to appease his wrath (34:5-7). "[The] smoke will rise for ever and ever" (34:8-10), and the lands will be left desolate (34:11-17; see also 32:12-14).

God's alien work

The second audience is Judah. Like Israel, they will face disaster. When measured against the plumb-line of God's righteousness, they are found wanting (**28:17**). So they will be swept away like debris in a flood (**28:17-19**). Despite their confidence in their alliance with Egypt, they are in fact ill-prepared for the Assyrian onslaught—like a man sleeping in a bed which is too short with a blanket that is too small (**28:20**). "The LORD will rise up as he did at Mount Perazim," says **28:21**; "he will rouse himself as in the Valley of Gibeon". Those were two occasions when God fought *for* his people (2 Samuel 5:17-21; Joshua 10:1-11). But now God will fight *against* his people. If the people continue to mock God rather than repent of their sin, their afflictions will be worse (Isaiah **28:22**).

So the people of Judah are no better than the people of Israel. Yet God graciously sustains them as his covenant people. One feature of God's grace is that he refines and purifies his people. To his people, what happens is fatherly discipline. And so we come to the key verse. God will send destruction...

"... to do his work, his strange work,
and perform his task, his alien task." (**28:21**)

God is at work. He has not gone AWOL. But what he's doing is "his strange work" and "his alien task".

This work seems strange to us because it's not what we want or expect. We think we know what God ought to be doing, and it's certainly not this illness, this redundancy, this hardship, this conflict. We can't understand what God is up to. It's not just that it doesn't fit with what we want. It doesn't seem to fit with some of the things the Bible says about God. God is a Father, but what kind of father makes his children ill? God is kind, so why does he send hardship into my life? God is love, so why does he allow so many people to take the road to hell? It seems God is being unkind and unloving.

> God is like a builder, demolishing so he can build something much better.

But all is not what it seems. God may destroy, but when he is dealing with his people, he destroys only so he can bring life. Yes, there can be a violence to God's work. Isaiah says God is like a builder demolishing a site (**28:17**). In **28:23-29** the imagery changes, and Isaiah talks about God ploughing up the ground and threshing the corn. But then Isaiah concludes:

"All this also comes from the LORD Almighty,
whose plan is wonderful,
whose wisdom is magnificent." (**28:29**)

Why is it wonderful when God sweeps through our lives in destruction or ploughs up our hearts? Because God is like a builder demolishing a site so he can build something much better. In **28:17-22** God sweeps away all false hope so we might put our hope on a firm foundation. Or God is like a farmer ploughing so he can plant. God's aim is to bring life. There may be times when it feels like God is ploughing up our hearts. But the result will be greater fruit.

"When a farmer ploughs for planting, does he plough continu-
ally?
Does he keep on breaking up and working the soil?
When he has levelled the surface,
does he not sow caraway and scatter cummin?
Does he not plant wheat in its place,
barley in its plot,
and spelt in its field?" (**28:24-25**)

God's aim is always to produce a harvest. "No discipline seems pleasant at the time, but painful," says Hebrews 12:11. "Later on, however, it produces a harvest of righteousness and peace for those who have been trained by it."

There is also a proportionality about God's strange work. It is carefully measured. God allows us to suffer no more than is required to achieve his purpose in our lives.

"Caraway is not threshed with a sledge,
nor is the cartwheel rolled over cummin;
caraway is beaten out with a rod,
and cummin with a stick.
Grain must be ground to make bread;
so one does not go on threshing it for ever.
The wheels of a threshing-cart may be rolled over it,
but one does not use horses to grind grain." (**28:27-28**)

The great Victorian preacher Charles Spurgeon comments:

"God gives us love without measure, but chastisement 'in measure' ... Every stroke is counted. It is the measure of wisdom,

the measure of sympathy, the measure of love, by which our discipline is regulated. Far be it from us to rebel against appointments so divine."

(Charles Spurgeon, *The Promises of God,* October 19th)

God's strange work is specific and tailored. It is like a carefully designed training programme. Each day God arranges the events of your life to make you a little bit more like Jesus. That's why Isaiah can say his plan is "wonderful" and "magnificent" (**28:29**).

Reader's guide

Isaiah 28

Isaiah 28 is the first in a series of "sermons" beginning with the word "Woe". It proclaims woe on the northern kingdom of Israel or Ephraim (28:1-13). But the real audience is the southern kingdom of Judah, with Jerusalem as its capital (28:14). In response to the threat of the Assyrian Empire, they were entering into a treaty with Egypt which Isaiah calls a "covenant with death" (28:15). As a result, God will do "his strange work" of using judgment to purify his people (28:17-29). But God promises to rebuild on "a precious **cornerstone***" (28:16)—a reference to Jesus (1 Peter 2:4-6).*

Isaiah 29

Isaiah proclaims woe to Jerusalem, which he terms "Ariel" (for reasons which are not clear). The city will be besieged (29:1-4) before the LORD delivers it (29:5-8)—a prophecy fulfilled when the Assyrian army surrounded the city (as Isaiah describes in chapter 36). But the people refuse to listen to Isaiah (29:9-12). In 29:15-16, those who think they can hide from the LORD are like pots which think they can manipulate the potter. Since the sighted refuse to see, God denounces their false worship (29:13). Jesus would quote these words to denounce the religious leaders of his day (Mark 7:5-8). Instead God will give sight to the blind (29:17-24). It's a promise fulfilled every time someone is **converted***, as God opens their eyes to see the glory of Christ.*

Isaiah 30

Isaiah says a treaty with Egypt is useless (30:1-7). But the people refuse to listen and instead ask Isaiah to proclaim pleasant things (30:8-11). So God says their trust in Egypt is like taking refuge in a wall that is about to collapse (30:12-14). True refuge is found in trusting God. For God longs to be gracious (30:15-22) and promises to rescue his people from the threat of Assyria (30:23-33). This is fulfilled in Isaiah 37 when King Hezekiah does turn to God and God does defeat the Assyrians.

Isaiah 31

Judah is turning to Egypt in the face of the Assyrian threat. But, while Egypt might look like a good option, the Egyptians are "mere mortals" (31:3) and "Assyria will fall by no human sword" (31:8). Instead the LORD will "pass over" as he did over Egypt to liberate his people (31:5).

Isaiah 32

*Through this section Isaiah has denounced the blindness and folly of the people. While God's ways are revealed to the humble (29:17-19; 30:19-22; 32:3-4), they remain hidden (29:9-12; 30:8-11) from the wise (29:14) and religious (29:13). "The ruthless will vanish, the mockers will disappear" (29:20-21; see also 32:9-13; 33:13-16). But now Isaiah says, "A king will reign in righteousness" (32:1—a reference to Jesus—and when he comes, the blind will see and fools will become wise (32:1-8). This promise was literally fulfilled when Jesus cured those who were blind, and it is metaphorically fulfilled whenever someone becomes a Christian. But first God will devastate the land of Judah (32:9-14), before renewing it when he pours out his Spirit (32:15-20). It's a promise partially fulfilled in the renewal of people in the church after **Pentecost** and ultimately fulfilled when God makes all things new.*

Isaiah 33

Once again Isaiah proclaims the futility of a treaty with Egypt (33:1, 7-14). But God also promises the renewal of his people (33:15-24).

"Your eyes will see the king in his beauty and view a land that stretches afar" (33:17). Rivers will bring trade to Jerusalem, but no warships will threaten it (33:21). At the moment Jerusalem is like an ill-prepared galleon, but in the future it will enjoy the spoils of victory (33:23). People's sickness will be healed and their sins will be forgiven (33:24). It is a vision which begins to be fulfilled with the first coming of Jesus and will be consummated at his second coming. In the meantime, Isaiah gives a prayer to pray and a promise to trust (33:2-6).

Isaiah 34

Using gruesome imagery, Isaiah proclaims God's final judgment on all nations (34:1-4). What happened to Edom in history is a sign of this (34:5-15). Its territory has been so depopulated that it now belongs to wild animals. The destruction of Edom will confirm Isaiah's words, and this will be a sign that what Isaiah says about the long-term future will also come to pass (34:16-17).

Isaiah 35

In chapter 34 God's judgment turned the world into a desert. But in chapter 35 God promises that the desert will bloom again (35:1-2). God will renew creation (35:1-7) and gather his people home (35:8-10). We have a preview of this future in the ministry of Jesus (Luke 7:21-22), but this promise will ultimately be fulfilled in the renewal of all things when Jesus returns in glory.

A sure foundation

So what do we do when God seems AWOL? How should we respond when we feel overwhelmed by the storms of life? Where do we turn when it feels like everything in which we take refuge is being swept away?

Don't take refuge in human strength—that doesn't work, as we saw in Isaiah **28:1-6**. Don't take refuge in human wisdom—that doesn't work either, as we saw in **28:7-13**. I wonder what this means for you. Where is your confidence placed? What is your hope for life?

What is your hope for life after death? What is the lie in which you're tempted to take refuge?

In chapter 28 only one thing is left standing:

"So this is what the Sovereign LORD says:
'See, I lay a stone in Zion, a tested stone,
    a precious cornerstone for a sure foundation;
the one who relies on it
    will never be stricken with panic.'" (**28:16**)

The New Testament says this cornerstone is Jesus (1 Peter 2:4-8). When everything else comes crashing down, the sure foundation is Jesus. God destroys so that he can build, and Jesus is the foundation and cornerstone of that building. What do you do when it feels like God has gone AWOL? You look to the cross. The cross is God's ultimate "strange work".

- The cross was an act of judgment that brought forgiveness.

- The cross was an act of abandonment that brought reconciliation.

- The cross was an act of shame that brought glory.

- The cross was an act of defeat that brought victory.

And so the cross is the great demonstration of God's faithfulness and God's love.

In the midst of the pain and confusion, it may seem as if God doesn't care. But look to the cross and see there the full extent of God's love. You may not be able to explain how God is at work in the current crisis that engulfs you. But you can trust that God is at work and that he is at work for your good. The LORD, says Isaiah in 33:5-6, "will be the sure foundation for your times, a rich store of salvation and wisdom and knowledge; the fear of the LORD is the key to this treasure".

Isaiah **28:16** says, "The one who relies on [God's cornerstone] will never be stricken with panic". It's literally "will never be hurried". The people of Judah were panicked, frenzied, hurried. They were scurrying off to Egypt in a desperate attempt to solve the problem posed by Assyria. We, too, can become panicked and frenzied when faced with a crisis. We feel the pressure to act, to perform, to solve. But in **28:12** God gave his people this invitation: "'This is the resting-place, let the weary rest'; and, 'This is the place of repose'". If the people had trusted God, they would have found rest and repose. But they would not trust God, and so they were in an almighty panic.

I wonder what "hurries" you? What puts you in a flap? What makes you over-busy? Your panic is almost certainly a sign of unbelief.

- You may be too busy because you are insecure and need to control life—when, in fact, God is great and cares for you as a **sovereign** heavenly Father.

- You may be too busy because you fear other people and so you can't say no—when, in fact, God is glorious and his opinion is that one that matters.

- You may be too busy because you're filling your life with activity in a desperate attempt to find satisfaction—when, in fact, God is good and the true source of joy.

- You may be too busy because you're trying to prove yourself through your work or your ministry—when, in fact, God is gracious and **justifies** you freely through faith in the finished work of Christ.

Here is Charles Spurgeon again:

"God's people will not be in a hurry to run away, for they shall not be overcome with the fear which causes panic. When others are flying here and there as if their wits had failed them, believers will be quiet, calm, and deliberate. And so they will be able to act wisely in the hour of testing.

"They will not be in a hurry with their expectations, craving their good things at once and on the spot. Instead they will wait God's time ...

"They will not be in a hurry to plunge into wrong or questionable actions. Unbelief must be doing something, and thus it works its own undoing. But faith makes no more haste than good speed ...

"What about me? Am I believing, and am I therefore keeping to the believer's pace, which is walking with God? Be at peace, fluttering spirit! Oh, rest in the Lord, and wait patiently for him!" (Charles Spurgeon, *The Promises of God*, November 29)

Questions for reflection

1. Do you find this passage comforting or worrying? Why?

2. How has God used suffering in your own life or the lives of those you love? How can you make sure you remember those times to help yourself keep going when you suffer in the future?

3. What will it look like for you to "[keep] to the believer's pace ... rest in the Lord, and wait patiently for him"?

7. GOD HEARS OUR PRAYERS

FOCUS: ISAIAH 37

In chapters 28 – 35, Judah has been faced with the threat posed by the Assyrian Empire, the rising superpower of the day under its king, Sennacherib. The instinct of many has been to seek help from Egypt. But Isaiah has declared, "Woe to those who go down to Egypt for help" (31:1) for Egypt is "utterly useless" (30:7). Instead, Isaiah has called on the people to trust the LORD for deliverance. In chapter 36 the Assyrian army arrives at the gates of Jerusalem, and Egypt is nowhere to be seen. In **37:1** Hezekiah tears his clothes and wears sackcloth in an apparent act of contrition for the nation's misplaced trust in Egypt—a policy now in tatters.

In Isaiah 36 – 39, we turn from prophetic oracle to historical narrative (in chapters that largely replicate 2 Kings 18:17 – 20:21). They tell the story of Hezekiah's magnificent trust in God and God's magnificent deliverance. For Isaiah's readers—then and now—these chapters therefore serve as a case study or worked example of the kind of faith to which Isaiah has been calling us.

Reader's guide

Isaiah 36

Sennacherib, the king of Assyria, invades Judah and besieges Jerusalem. His army commander says resistance is useless and faith in the LORD is futile.

Isaiah 37

Hezekiah, the king of Judah, seeks help from the prophet Isaiah (37:1-7). After a brief respite (37:8), Sennacherib renews his threats (37:9-13). So Hezekiah turns to God in prayer (37:14-20). Isaiah predicts Sennacherib's downfall (37:21-35). The angel of the LORD kills 185,000 members of the Assyrian army, which therefore withdraws, and some time later Sennacherib is assassinated by his own sons (37:36-38).

Isaiah 38

King Hezekiah becomes ill and Isaiah says his illness will end in his death (38:1). So Hezekiah prays to God and God grants him an extra fifteen years of life (38:2-8). Hezekiah responds with a hymn of praise (38:9-22).

Isaiah 39

King Hezekiah receives a delegation from Babylon and shows them all his treasures. The prophet Isaiah is angry when he finds out what has happened and predicts the defeat of Judah by Babylon. This predication was fulfilled a century or so later when the Babylonian Empire under King Nebuchadnezzar destroyed Jerusalem and plundered Judah.

The Assyrian army has invaded Judah, capturing the fortified cities in the north (Isaiah 36:1). What Isaiah's account does not include is the fact that Hezekiah initially tried to buy off Sennacherib by presenting him with a tribute of gold and silver, much of it taken from the temple in Jerusalem (2 Kings 18:13-16). This appears to have rather backfired on Hezekiah, for instead of quenching Sennacherib's thirst, it seems to have fuelled it. From his current centre of operations at Lachish, Sennacherib now sends his field commander (backed by "a large army") to meet a delegation of officials from King Hezekiah (Isaiah 36:2-3).

The action begins with a war of words. Judah may talk a good talk when it comes to war, says the Assyrian commander, but it's all "empty words" (36:4-5). They may think they can depend on Egypt, but Egypt will not deliver them. Imagine you're under attack, so you grab a stick to defend yourself, but the stick turns out to be just a splintered reed. Not only is it unable to fend off your assailant; it leaves splinters in your hand. *That's what Egypt is like,* says the field commander. This claim is true and echoes what Isaiah has already told the people. The commander's second claim, however, is not true: *nor can you depend on the LORD,* he says, *because King Hezekiah has just removed his high places*—religious shrines that God had forbidden (36:7). The commander's knowledge of current affairs was good, for Hezekiah had recently destroyed the high places in Judah (2 Kings 18:4). But his knowledge of theology was terrible. Far from offending the LORD, the removal of the high places had delighted him (18:5-6). But you can imagine how this claim might have sown doubt in the minds of many in Jerusalem, especially those wary of Hezekiah's religious reforms. The commander's third line of attack is a straight taunt. *I'll give you a head start,* he

> The commander's knowledge of current affairs was good. But his theology was terrible.

says in effect. He mockingly offers Judah 2,000 horses to even things up a bit. But he knows Judah lacks the resources to provide them with riders (Isaiah 36:8-9). His fourth approach is another lie: he claims to have divine sanction from the LORD to destroy Judah (36:10).

The location of this meeting at the Upper Pool is significant, for we have been here before. This is where Isaiah had met King Ahaz (Hezekiah's father) in 7:3. Back then God had offered to rescue King Ahaz from the threat posed by Aram and the northern tribes of Israel, but Ahaz had chosen instead to look for help from Assyria. Now Assyria has become the threat. Ahaz's son, Hezekiah, faces a similar dilemma: to trust in God or seek help from elsewhere (with Egypt as the top option). The prophet Isaiah's first words to the son in **37:6**—"Do not be afraid"—repeat his message to the father in 7:4. King Ahaz chose to trust in Assyrian assistance, and it has ended with the Assyrian army camped on Jerusalem's front lawn. We are about to discover what happens when we choose to trust God.

King Hezekiah's delegation asks the commander to speak in Aramaic so that the Hebrew-speaking people of Jerusalem will not understand (36:11). Aramaic was the language of international diplomacy, so it was not an unreasonable request. But instead the Assyrian commander shouts defiantly to the city walls (36:12). The commander insists that Hezekiah is wrong to claim that God will help Judah (36:13-15). The phrase "everyone under their own vine and under their own fig tree" had once described the high point of Israel's life under King Solomon (1 Kings 4:25). Echoing this language, the commander promises that Assyria will create a new golden age (Isaiah 36:16-17). But make no mistake: despite all the talk of peace, this is a call for complete submission. The Assyrian commander's final argument is perhaps his strongest: the formidable track record of the Assyrian army. Just like Judah, other nations thought their gods would save them—but "have the gods of any nations ever delivered their lands from the hand of the king of Assyria?" (36:18-20) The people of Judah have nothing to say in response (36:21-22).

The theology of Assyria is clear. No god can stand against the power of the Assyrian military machine. Besides which, removing shrines—as Hezekiah has done—is inevitably going to anger a god, because gods demand to be served. It's striking, though, that Assyrian gods are not mentioned: Sennacherib's faith is in himself and his army. In 36:15-17 the commander calls on the people of Jerusalem to put their faith in the peace promised by Sennacherib rather than to put their faith in the deliverance promised by the LORD. This is the Assyrian claim: Sennacherib is more powerful than the LORD, and his word is more trustworthy.

Hezekiah sees clearly that the issue is the LORD's reputation: "It may be that the LORD your God will hear the words of the field commander, whom his master, the king of Assyria, has sent to ridicule the living God, and that he will rebuke him for the words the LORD your God has heard" (**37:4**). Hezekiah goes to the temple to pray and sends officials to the prophet Isaiah (**37:1-4**). Isaiah reassures Hezekiah (**37:5-6**). A report will come leading to the withdrawal of the Assyrian army (**37:7**). The LORD, too, recognises that at stake is his reputation: "This is what the LORD says: Do not be afraid of what you have heard—those words with which the underlings of the king of Assyria have **blasphemed** me" (**37:6**).

There is a short lull in the war of words as the Assyrian commander withdraws to assist Sennacherib, who's now moved on to Libnah (**37:8**). But it proves to be only a temporary respite. A report comes to Sennacherib, just as Isaiah has predicted, suggesting a threat from Egypt (**37:9**). It seems this prompts Sennacherib to increase the pressure on Hezekiah with the hope of wrapping up his Judean campaign swiftly. So Sennacherib himself resumes the threats against Jerusalem, sending a letter to Hezekiah demanding submission (**37:9-13**).

Hezekiah's God

Hezekiah responds by spreading the letter out before God in the temple. Hezekiah begins his prayer: "LORD Almighty, the God of Israel, enthroned between the **cherubim**, you alone are God over all the kingdoms of the earth. You have made heaven and earth" (**37:16**). It's easy to think of sentiments like this as "filler": stock phrases to pad out our prayers. Or perhaps we think of them as the warm-up before we get to the important content of our requests. But remember the situation that Hezekiah is facing. Assyria was the great superpower of the day. A long list of kings had already fallen to her army (36:18-20). Judah's own fortified cities had been destroyed (36:1). Imagine that a battalion of enemy army tanks is crowded outside your house, backed by air support, and all you have is a baseball bat! Faced with the Assyrian war machine, Judah was powerless. Consider the content of Sennacherib's letter in **37:10-13**. Here's a paraphrase of his argument: *It's no use thinking your God will save you. Gozan, Harran, Rezeph,*

Eden, Hamath, Arpad, Lair, Sepharvaim, Hena, Ivvah—all these cities thought their god would save them. But where are they now? Why do you think you'll be any different?

Why indeed? It's a powerful argument, and Hezekiah acknowledges its force. "It is true, LORD," he says in **37:18**, "that the Assyrian kings have laid waste all these peoples and their lands."

Despite the powerful claims of the Assyrians, Hezekiah still has confidence in God—a confidence that drives his praying. Assyria may have defeated other nations and their gods, but there are four big differences this time around.

1. *The almighty God.* Jerusalem's God is "the LORD Almighty" (**37:16**), and there are no limitations to his power. Sennacherib may have the numbers on his side—so much so that his commander can spare 2,000 horses and still be confident of victory (36:8). But, as Gideon discovered, when the LORD is on your side, numbers count for very little (Judges 6 – 7). Indeed, "the LORD Almighty" is literally "the LORD of hosts", which reminds us that God has angelic armies at his disposal (2 Kings 6:15-17). In Isaiah 36:14 Sennacherib's commander had said, "This is what the king say …" Isaiah responds, "This is what the LORD says…" (**37:6**). The commander had called Sennacherib "the great king" (36:13). Throughout the known world, what Sennacherib said was done. But now a greater King has spoken.

2. *The only God.* Unlike other gods, the LORD is not some national deity. He is "God over all the kingdoms of the earth" (**37:16**). When Sennacherib comes against Judah, it is not Assyria's gods versus another nation's gods. That was what was going on with the other nations—or at least that's how Sennacherib saw it. But when Sennacherib came against Judah, he was coming against the one true God—the God who is "alone" (**37:16**).

3. *The living God.* The LORD is the one who "made heaven and earth" (**37:16**). By contrast, other gods are made. The Assyrians have defeated other gods, but "they were not gods but only

wood and stone, fashioned by human hands" (**37:19**). Isaiah is anticipating here his mockery of idols in 44:9-20. The gods of the nations are "not gods" at all, but the God of Israel is "the living God" (**37:4, 17**).

4. *The merciful God.* The LORD is "enthroned between the cherubim" (**37:16**). This is more than simply a claim that God in heaven is encircled by angels. This is a very specific location. The **ark** in the tabernacle and temple had two cherubim on top. The ark shared the same dimensions as the footstool of a royal throne. In other words, while God's throne was in heaven, the ark was his footstool on earth (66:1). But "between the cherubim" was not only the place of divine rule; it was also the place of divine mercy. For between the cherubim was "the atonement cover" (Exodus 35:12)—the place where atonement was made by the high priest on the Day of Atonement (Leviticus 16:15-16). Other gods make demands, but the LORD shows mercy.

Here are four reasons to think that Sennacherib's track record of victory over other nations counts for nothing when he confronts "the God of Israel" (Isaiah **37:16**). Think of the forces that give you cause for concern. Think of the people whom you fear—those people whose acceptance you crave or whose rejection you fear. Think of the threats to the church in the West or the nations which persecute God's people around the world. And now compare them to our God: the LORD Almighty, God over all, the Maker of heaven and earth, and the God of atoning mercy. This is the only true antidote to fear. It may not be a cure that works overnight; you may need to keep reminding yourself of who God is, and you may need to keep coming back to his word. But this is what will calm your heart in a crisis and correct your perspective over time.

Hezekiah spreads out the letter in the temple (**37:14**). It's not that Hezekiah is providing God with information of which God is unaware. It's a kind of an enacted prayer. But it also works on Hezekiah's heart. It's a deliberate act through which Hezekiah brings his problem tangibly "before the LORD". It's a practice you might find helpful from time to time. When something is concerning or disturbing you, find some physical embodiment of your problem (like a letter) and "spread it out before the LORD". Matching that act with the kind of praise Hezekiah offers in **37:16** may help you get your problem into perspective. "Cast all your anxiety on him," says 1 Peter 5:7, "because he cares for you".

Questions for reflection

1. Have you ever faced ridicule or attack for your faith like that in the speech in Isaiah 36? Looking back, to what degree do you think God's reputation and name was the main issue for your attacker? What about for you?

2. How do you address God when you pray? What difference would it make to pray more like Hezekiah?

3. How else can you keep reminding yourself of what God is like?

PART TWO

King Hezekiah is facing perhaps the greatest challenge of his life. He responds, first, by reminding himself of who God as he turns to God in praise. He looks beyond his circumstances to see the bigger picture: the sovereign power of God.

God's glory

Hezekiah then invites God to take note of what's happening: "Give ear, LORD, and hear; open your eyes, LORD, and see; listen to all the words Sennacherib has sent to ridicule the living God" (**37:17**). Notice the five injunctions: "give ear … hear … open your eyes … see … listen". Hezekiah is drawing God's attention to the situation. But the situation in question is not so much the plight of Jerusalem (though that is implicit) but the honour of God. This emphasis is reflected again in the climax of the prayer as Hezekiah makes his core request: "Now, LORD our God, deliver us from his hand, so that all the kingdoms of the earth may know that you, LORD, are the only God" (**37:20**). It's a request for deliverance, but primarily it's a request for God to defend his honour and magnify his name.

Look at this, LORD, Hezekiah is saying in effect. *Your name is being dishonoured; your reputation is on the line; your ways are being ridiculed.* Do your prayers reflect this kind of concern for God's glory? All the way through this story the key issue is God's reputation. It's a concern we meet again in the Lord's Prayer: "**hallowed** be your name". Jesus taught us to begin by asking God to honour his name. Is that the starting point for your prayers?

This prayer is also a missionary prayer. What Hezekiah wants is for *the nations* to know God as Hezekiah knows him—"so that all the kingdoms of the earth may know that you, LORD, are the only God" (**37:20**). The best way to pray for the glory of God is to pray for the mission of the church. And the best argument when we pray for the mission of the church is the glory of God. We pray for people to turn from the rejection of God to the worship of God.

Sometimes our prayers can be a bit like running through a check-list. Family. "Lord, please bless my family." Tick. Church. "And please bless our church." Tick. Health. Tick. Mission. Tick. Job done. On to the next task of the day. But Hezekiah gives us a model for "arguing" with God in prayer. Of course, we can't manipulate God. But, like other prayers recorded in the Bible, this prayer not only makes requests to God; it also presents arguments to God. Sometimes Bible pray-ers argue on the basis of the *promises* of God or the *mercy* of God. But here the argument centres around the *glory* of God.

What might it mean to pray in this way? Suppose you are praying for an **evangelistic** enterprise. You might say:

*Father God, we pray for our guest service on Sunday. You have promised to gather your people from across the earth (11:12; 43:5; 56:8). You have promised that your word will not return to you empty (55:10-11). You have promised that you will justify many people through the work of Christ (53:11). Fulfil your promises among us, we pray. Glorify your name in the lives of people as they turn to you in faith. Today your name is so often simply used as a swear word. Through our guest service, may there be people who start to use your name in a new way: to praise you for your salvation (12:4). Deliver people from Satan's power, so that everyone may know that you, LORD, are the only God (**37:20**).*

Or suppose you're praying for a sick friend. You might say:

Father God, we don't know whether it's your will to heal George or not, but we know Christ has promised to carry his people close to his heart (40:11). Comfort George with the comfort of your word and fill him with the hope of eternity (40:1-2). Glorify your name through George. We pray that people will see your hope within him and be drawn to find out more about your ways (2:2-5). We pray that his faith may shine brightly to the

*medical staff and to his family (60:1-3). Do this, Father, for the
sake of your holy name (**37:35**).*

Sennacherib's downfall

God's response to Hezekiah's prayer comes in three parts: one addressed to Sennacherib (**37:21-29**); one addressed to Hezekiah
(**37:30-32**); and one about Sennacherib (**37:33-35**). Once again, the
key issue is the fact that Sennacherib has insulted God:

"Who is it you have insulted and blasphemed?
Against whom have you raised your voice and lifted your
eyes in pride?
Against the Holy One of Israel!
By your messengers you have ridiculed the Lord." (**37:23-24**)

Isaiah reprises the message he spoke against Assyria in chapter 10.
Sennacherib claims he has "ascended the heights" of the geopolitical stage through his own power (10:7-11, 13-14; **37:23-25**), but in
reality he's simply a tool in God's hands (10:5-6, 15; **37:26-27**). And
now, because he has failed to honour God, he'll get a taste of his own
medicine (10:16-19; **37:28-29**). In **37:33** Isaiah promises that the Assyrians will not enter Jerusalem (which is why she's called a "Virgin" in
37:22). Instead, Sennacherib will go home in disgrace (**37:34**).

To Hezekiah God promises national renewal; the economy will
recover (**37:30**) and a faithful remnant of God's people will emerge
(**37:31-32**). It's a promise for the next three years (**37:30**), but the
promise of the remnant will take on renewed significance when God's
people find themselves in Babylonian exile.

The second oracle ends, "The zeal of the LORD Almighty will accomplish this" (**37:32**), while the third ends, "I will defend this city
and save it, for my sake and for the sake of David my servant!"
(**37:35**) God is zealous. He is passionate about his glory. And so he
will save Jerusalem "for my sake"—that is, to vindicate the honour
of his reputation. He will also save Jerusalem "for the sake of David

my servant"—that is, to fulfil his promise that one of David's sons would always reign over God's people (2 Samuel 7:15-16).

What Isaiah promised duly happened: "Then the angel of the LORD went out and put to death a hundred and eighty-five thousand in the Assyrian camp. When the people got up the next morning—there were all the dead bodies!" (Isaiah **37:36**) Sennacherib returns home in disgrace and is later assassinated by his sons (**37:37-38**), just as Isaiah had foretold (**37:7, 29, 34**).

The remarkable thing about this account of Jerusalem's deliverance is how brief it is! It was an astonishing act and one full of dramatic possibilities. But it's covered in an almost cursory way (**37:36**). What makes this even more striking is that, in setting the scene, the writer includes three extended descriptions of Assyrian provocation (36:1-10, 11-22; **37:9-13**). We want him to balance these out with an extended description of Sennacherib's comeuppance. But perhaps the point is to stress Hezekiah's faith in the face of dire threat. Three times we have been given compelling reasons as to why submitting to Assyria makes sense. But still Hezekiah trusts God—and this leads to God's glory. Hezekiah's prayer in **37:20** is answered; all the kingdoms of the earth do learn that the LORD is the only God. It's a prayer which is still being answered today as you read these words!

Recovery and fall

Hezekiah becomes extremely ill and Isaiah advises him to prepare for death (38:1). Hezekiah, though, prays for deliverance with bitter tears (38:2-3), and so God promises to add 15 extra years to his life (38:4-6, 21-22). To confirm this promise, God gives a sign: the shadow of the sun retreats ten steps (38:7-8). We're not told how this sign was accomplished, although 2 Chronicles 32:31 suggests it was a local phenomenon within the land of Judah. God, as it were, turns back time in one day, just as he will do in Hezekiah's life. Hezekiah responds with a song (Isaiah 38:9). He begins by describing the threat to his life posed by his illness in a powerful series of images depicting human frailty (38:10-14). Then Hezekiah celebrates God's restoration: "You restored me to health and let me live" (38:16).

Hezekiah cites two reasons for his recovery. First, he says, "In your love you kept me from the pit of destruction; you have put all my sins behind your back" (38:17). "The wages of sin is death," says Paul in Romans 6:23. But Hezekiah receives life instead of death because God has overlooked his sins. For Hezekiah this was a temporary measure. But it points to the ultimate and enduring solution for sin when Christ would pay the penalty of sin on the cross. The solution provided by Christ would lead not just to 15 extra years of life but eternal life for all who belong to him. In his request Hezekiah points to his own faithfulness (Isaiah 38:3), but in his praise he recognises that our real hope is in God's faithfulness (38:18-19).

> Hezekiah recognises that our real hope is in God's faithfulness.

Second, Hezekiah's recovery brings praise to God: "For the grave cannot praise you, death cannot sing your praise … The living, the living—they praise you, as I am doing today" (38:18-20). Again, for Hezekiah this was only temporary. But when those who are in Christ are raised to eternal life, we will praise God for ever. Hezekiah's passion for God's glory will extend into coming ages.

Hezekiah also gives one reason for his original illness: "Surely it was for my benefit,", he says in 38:17, "that I suffered such anguish". Perhaps Hezekiah saw his illness as an act of divine discipline. Perhaps he discovered more of God's grace in bringing undeserved life in the place of deserved death. But perhaps also Hezekiah is looking to us at this point. Hezekiah's story has a place in the message of the book of Isaiah because Hezekiah is a picture of God's people. The first readers of Isaiah are facing exile in Babylon. Will this be the end of the story? Will this be the death of God's people? No, because God can restore people to health and let them live (38:16). Why? Because one day, in his love, he will deal with sin completely through Jesus and create a people who will praise him for ever.

At this point those following Isaiah's ministry might be wondering whether Hezekiah is the shoot promised from the stump of Jesse, who will reign over the nations (11:1). After all, he has seen off the world's superpower, and he has come back from the brink of death. But his story ends in tragedy. Hezekiah receives envoys from Babylon. They have heard of his miraculous recovery and bring a gift to honour him (39:1). Though the text doesn't say so explicitly, it seems that Hezekiah's success has gone to his head. In his pride he shows them all his splendours (39:2). It may have been part of negotiating a pact with Babylon—the kind of pact that his father had disastrously made with Assyria and that he himself may have made with Egypt. (Marduk-Baladan led a decade-long revolt against Assyria and may have wanted Hezekiah's support.)

Isaiah is certainly suspicious (39:3). "What did they see?" he asks. "'They saw everything in my palace,' Hezekiah said. 'There is nothing among my treasures that I did not show them'" (39:4). In response Isaiah says that a time is coming when everything will be carried off into exile in Babylon—both possessions and people (39:5-7). Five times the word "everything" is used. 39:2 is literally "Hezekiah ... showed them ... *everything* in his armoury and *everything* found among his treasures. There was nothing in his palace or among *everything* in his kingdom that Hezekiah did not show them." We meet the word "everything" again in 39:4 and 39:6. Hezekiah has shown the Babylonians everything and so everything, will be carried away to Babylon as plunder.

This forms a poignant postscript to Hezekiah's story. "Hezekiah trusted in the LORD, the God of Israel," says 2 Kings 18:5. "There was no one like him among all the kings of Judah, either before him or after him." It is the highest possible praise. Yet Hezekiah was not the messianic king who would restore God's reign over the earth. Instead, his story ends with a sense of foreboding. It prepares us for the remainder of the book of Isaiah, in which Isaiah addresses those caught up in the exile that Hezekiah has precipitated. After reading Isaiah 36 – 37, we might ask, "Why did Judah end up in exile when

God could respond to their faith with such remarkable acts of deliverance?" What chapters 38 – 39 remind us of is that the faith shown in chapters 36 – 37 was the exception rather than the norm. The scene is set for Isaiah's prophecy of the Servant of God, who will end the exile and restore God's reign (40:1-11).

Questions for reflection

1. How might it alter what you pray if you make God's glory and reputation central to your prayers?

2. What feels familiar or relatable in the way Hezekiah talks about his illness and recovery? Does anything surprise you?

3. In what area of life do you most need faith like Hezekiah's at the moment?

8. THE COMING OF GOD

FOCUS: ISAIAH 40:1-11

Imagine you live in a comfortable house in a pleasant town. You run a small business. It's often hard work, but you enjoy the rewards of your labour. You're able to provide for your children, and the future looks secure. It's probably not too hard for most of us to imagine this because it more or less describes our lives.

Until the day the soldiers arrive. There are shouts in the streets. Cries of alarm. And then your door bursts open, and men with weapons spill in. You can take whatever you can carry. But be warned: it's a 700-mile journey through the desert. According to Google Maps it takes 225 hours on foot—and you're going to be on foot. The soldiers are shouting. The children are crying. And you're trying to think of what to take.

Worldwide, over 65 million people have been forced to leave their home—that's getting on for one in a hundred people on the planet. 15 million of those people have been forced to leave their country.

The prophet Isaiah was writing to refugees in chapters 40 – 55: refugees who had seen their homeland torn apart; who had been dragged away into exile; who had wept by the rivers of Babylon; who had no heart to sing the songs of their homeland (Psalm 137:1-4). Isaiah wrote in the 8th century BC. But here he looks forward 200 years to the coming exile in Babylon.

Isaiah begins his message to these distraught refugees with words of comfort: "Comfort, comfort my people, says your God" (**40:1**).

What comfort is there for refugees? What is Isaiah's good news? The answer comes in **40:9**: "Here is your God!"

Reader's guide

Isaiah 40

In 587 BC Jerusalem was destroyed by the Babylonian Empire, and the people of Judah were carried away into exile—as Isaiah had proph-esied. In chapters 40 – 55 Isaiah looks forward to address these exiles. He begins with words of "comfort" (40:1-2). The good news is that God is going to come to his people to bring them home (40:3-11). It is a prediction of the end to exile in Babylon, but it also points forward to an end to humanity's exile from God. God can do this because he is far greater than the nations (40:12-31).

Isaiah 41

In 41:1-4 God calls someone from the east to defeat Babylon. This is a reference to Cyrus, the king who would defeat the Babylonian Empire and who we will meet again in 44:24 – 45:4. The nations tremble with fear, but God's people no longer need to fear (41:5-16), for God will renew them (41:17-20). God calls the nations and their gods to a court case which will lead to their exposure (41:1, 21-24). God pre-dicts the coming of "one from the north" (41:25)—another reference to Cyrus. Among the "gods", only the LORD can make this kind of prediction (41:25-28): "See, they are all false! Their deeds amount to nothing; their images are but wind and confusion" (41:29).

Isaiah 42

Isaiah introduces the Servant of the LORD, who will redeem God's peo-ple and bring light to the nations (42:1-9). This is ultimately Jesus. Isaiah invites everyone from across the earth to praise God (42:10-12) because God himself is going to march forth like a warrior to rescue (42:13-17). This is a promise fulfilled when Jesus marches forth from heaven to rescue us. Yet still people continue to be blind to Isaiah's message (42:18-25).

What Isaiah's readers faced was not just a political crisis but a spiritual crisis: a crisis of faith. Perhaps the God in whom we trusted is powerless. Perhaps the forces of international geopolitics are beyond his control. Or perhaps God has abandoned us. Perhaps he merely looks on from afar, indifferent to our plight. Where is God? Maybe you're asking questions like that—whether you're a refugee or not. Isaiah says, *Here is God.*

"Here is your God!" in **40:9** is literally "See your God". That word "see" is then repeated in **40:10**. "See your God. See, the Sovereign LORD comes with power ... See, his reward is with him." In other words, **40:10-11** explains why God is good news. Isaiah says in effect, *Look to God, and let me tell you what he's going to do. See God and see him in action.* What we discover is that God is good news because God comes, God rewards and God gathers.

God comes

"See, the Sovereign LORD comes with power," says **40:10**, "and he rules with a mighty arm". It might look like the gods of Babylon are stronger. Today it might look like **secularism** or Islam is going to win the day. But God is coming, and he is coming with power.

Isaiah is summarising in **40:10** what he said in **40:3-4**:

"A voice of one calling:
 'In the wilderness prepare
   the way for the LORD;
 make straight in the desert
   a highway for our God.
 Every valley shall be raised up,
   every mountain and hill made low;
 the rough ground shall become level,
   the rugged places a plain.'"

Isaiah hears a voice, and the voice is calling for a construction project. Think of roads through mountainous areas. They hug the contours of the slopes. Sometimes there's a bridge across a valley; sometimes a cutting has been blasted through the mountain. All this civil engineering combines to ensure that you can drive on a flat, fast road. That's what the voice is calling for: raise the valleys, lower the hills, level the rough ground to make a flat, fast highway.

Who travels along this highway? It's God. God is coming to *rescue* his people and *reveal* his glory. "And the glory of the LORD will be revealed, and all people will see it together" (**40:5**). When the LORD, the God of Israel, arrives, everyone will know that he is God. "Here is God," we will say as Isaiah does in **40:9**. "Look, it's God."

> Israel's exile was always a pointer to something bigger: humanity's exile from God.

It may be that Isaiah has in mind a processional route. Before a royal event today, roads are swept, banners are hung and barriers are erected. Everything is prepared so the royal carriage can parade through the streets. Here in Isaiah the call goes out to prepare the route for the coming of the King: the ultimate King, God himself, coming to rule his people. "He rules with a mighty arm," says **40:10**.

For the exiles in Babylon, this was good news. God was coming to rescue them. God was coming to replace Babylonian rule with divine rule. But Israel's exile was always a pointer to something bigger and deeper, which is *humanity's exile from God*. Ever since we were expelled from the Garden of Eden with cherubim stationed there to prevent our return (Genesis 3:24), we have lived in exile. We are restless and rootless, cut off from God. But here is good news: "The Sovereign LORD comes with power, and he rules with a mighty arm" (Isaiah **40:10**). God is coming to lead us home.

Isaiah **40:3-5** may well sound familiar; for Mark opens his Gospel by quoting these words: "A voice of one calling in the wilderness, 'Prepare the way for the Lord'" (Mark 1:3). Mark quotes Isaiah **40:3** and then says, "And so **John the Baptist** appeared in the wilderness" (Mark 1:4). In other words, the "voice" is the voice of John the Baptist. And that means the Sovereign LORD coming to his people is Jesus. That's Mark's big point. The God who comes with power to rule is Jesus. The God who comes to rescue his people and reveal his glory is Jesus. We see Jesus feeding the poor, healing the sick, welcoming outcasts, touching lepers; and Isaiah says, "Here is your God!" Here is Jesus.

This is the good news we preach. God is not impotent; nor is he indifferent. For God has come in the person of his Son to lead us home.

God rewards

In Isaiah **40:10b** there is another call to "see": "See, his reward is with him, and his recompense accompanies him". Probably the idea here is that God comes with the spoils of battle. Here is the King, coming in triumphal procession, and he brings with him the plunder of war. Both the words "reward" and "recompense" are used to speak of "wages". This is the reward that God has earned. Or perhaps we should think in terms of Jesus, the Servant of the LORD. In Isaiah 49:4 the Servant of the LORD says, "Yet what is due to me is in the LORD'S hand, and my reward is with my God". Jesus will receive from God the reward that his work deserves, and he is coming to share that reward with his people. Isaiah 53:12 says that Jesus the Servant will divide the spoils of victory with his people.

Again, here in **40:10** Isaiah is echoing what he's already said in chapter 40. He talked about reward and payment in **40:1-2**:

"Comfort, comfort my people,
    says your God.
Speak tenderly to Jerusalem,
    and proclaim to her
that her hard service has been completed,
    that her sin has been paid for,
that she has received from the LORD'S hand
    double for all her sins."

We have three parallel statements: her punishment is complete; her sin is paid; she has received double. "Double" here doesn't mean that God has demanded twice what is owed. That would be unjust and cruel, and God is neither. It's more the idea of matching. The debt has its double—it has been matched by the payment that is made. So the sin of God's people has been paid for. The punishment is complete. It is finished.

Is that right? In one sense, yes. God had said Israel would spend 70 years in exile and those 70 years would come to an end. The punishment that God had decreed—70 years of exile—would reach its end. And yet, after their return, the Jews still felt like they were in exile. The underlying problem of sin still remained. Could 70 years wipe the slate clean? Could it really pay the price of sin—a price that thousands of animal sacrifices had failed to pay in any enduring sense? The answer is no.. Human beings can never repay the debt we owe to God. We can never recompense the price of sin.

But Isaiah has another answer. The word "sin" in **40:2** is the word translated "iniquity" in 53:5-6. Isaiah talks there of the Servant of the LORD—of the Lord Jesus Christ: "He was crushed for our *iniquities* ... and the LORD has laid on him the *iniquity* of us all." The reason Isaiah could speak comfort to the exiles was that God was coming in the person of his Son to pay the price of our sin.

In **40:2** the Servant—Jesus—comes to receive the wages that our sin deserves. And what are the wages of sin? Death (Romans 6:23). In **40:10** he comes to share the wages that his obedience deserves. And what is his reward? Life. This point is this: *we receive his reward of life because he received our reward of death.* We get what he deserves—life—because he took what we deserve—death.

Jesus himself said, "Blessed are those who mourn" (Matthew 5:4). In other words, blessed are those who feel the weight of their sin and who grieve the way they've treated God. Blessed are those who don't hide their sin or excuse their sin but confess it to God in repentance and faith. Jesus continues, "Blessed are those who mourn, *for they will be comforted*" (emphasis added). The comfort that Isaiah promised in **40:1** is fulfilled in Jesus. The Sovereign LORD has come in the person of Jesus to pay the price of sin through his death. And he has come to share the spoils of victory through his resurrection.

That is good news! Indeed, there is no better news. It's news worth shouting about. "Lift up your voice with a shout," says **40:9**. "Lift up your voice," says Isaiah, and "do not be afraid".

I find that a challenge. My temptation is to *lower* my voice—to keep quiet—because I'm afraid. So I often share the message of Christ as if it's bad news—as if I'm passing on a bad smell or asking a big favour. And, yes, the gospel is a call to repentance. For some it may be a call to die as a martyr. For all of us it is a call to die to self. But the gospel is good news. There's a clue in the name—it's *good* news! Our message is a word of comfort.

- To people exiled from God, we have good news of a way back home.

- To people feeling the shame of their guilt, we have good news of comfort.

- To people facing the wages of sin, we have good news that the price is paid.

- To people feeling abandoned, we have good news for God has come in the person of Jesus.

We have good news. So let's pass it on as news that is good—as if it's a secret to treasure, a declaration of victory, an announcement of reward, a way to be rescued.

Questions for reflection

1. When have you felt that God is far away? Perhaps you do now. How could you use this passage to encourage yourself in those times?

2. Think about specific people you know. What aspect of the "comfort" in this passage do they especially need to hear?

3. How will you "lift up your voice" in the coming weeks?

PART TWO

This is our good news: God comes in Christ, and God rewards in Christ. But we're not quite done yet, for God also gathers.

God gathers

Isaiah **40:11** says, "He tends his flock like a shepherd: he gathers the lambs in his arms and carries them close to his heart; he gently leads those that have young". We have four statements in this verse, each of which begins with a verb. This is what God does: he tends, he gathers, he carries, he leads. It's all very intimate. In **40:9** "he rules with a mighty arm". His arm there is a picture of power. It represents his ability to execute his reign. But in **40:11** "he gathers the lambs in his arm". It's a picture of tenderness and care.

In Revelation 7 the apostle John sees people from "every nation, tribe, people and language" standing round the throne of the Lamb, wearing white robes (Revelation 7:9). The question is asked, *Who are these people in white robes?* One of the elders says they are those who have "come out of the great **tribulation**" (Revelation 7:13-14). That's a way of describing the chaos and suffering of history. He's talked about war, famine and disease—the kind of horrors faced by the exiles in Babylon and by refugees today. John has talked, too, about the persecution of Christians. Revelation then picks up the promise of Isaiah 25:8 and combines it with the promise of a Shepherd-King gently leading his people in **40:11** to say:

"'Never again will they hunger;
        never again will they thirst.
The sun will not beat down on them,'
        nor any scorching heat.
For the Lamb at the centre of the throne
        will be their shepherd;
'he will lead them to springs of living water.'

'And God will wipe away every tear from their eyes.'"

(Revelation 7:16-17)

Jesus described himself as the Good Shepherd. Perhaps Isaiah 40 was one of the passages he had in mind when he did so (along with Psalm 23 and Ezekiel 34). God has come in power to pay the price of sin at the cross and share his new life through the resurrection. And now he gathers his people through the mission of the church. The Good Shepherd "calls his own sheep by name ... and his sheep follow him because they know his voice" (John 10:3-4). This is how Jesus gathers his sheep. You speak, and people hear the voice of Jesus. No wonder Isaiah says, "Lift up your voice". When you lift up your voice, for some people it will be the voice of the Good Shepherd. What goes in their ears might be the sound of your voice, talking about Jesus over a cup of tea. But what they hear will be the voice of the Good Shepherd.

A few years ago my wife and I visited missionaries in the Middle-East. There we saw shepherds walking across the hillsides with their flocks trailing along behind them. When they called, their sheep followed them. That's the image Jesus has in mind. That's what is happening in your evangelism. That is why Jesus sends us out in mission. That is why he sends you to your friends and neighbours. Jesus may send some of us to the ends of the earth. Why? So that he can gather his sheep.

So Jesus gathers his sheep through his word as we proclaim that word. In **40:6-8** Isaiah tells us something about the nature of that word:

"A voice says, 'Cry out.'
And I said, 'What shall I cry?'
'All people are like grass,
and all their faithfulness is like the flowers of the field.
The grass withers and the flowers fall,
because the breath of the LORD blows on them.
Surely the people are grass.

The grass withers and the flowers fall,
    but the word of our God endures for ever.'"

Human achievements come and go. Kingdoms rise, and kingdoms fall. At the beginning of Isaiah's ministry, Assyria was the emerging regional superpower. But he lived to see its defeat. At the end of his ministry, Isaiah looked ahead to announce Babylon as the coming imperial power. But he also predicted that it, too, would eventually fall. Over the centuries other regimes have come and gone. Ideologies have risen to prominence, some hell-bent on destroying the church. But God's word endures to this day.

Again, these verses may sound familiar. That is because Peter quotes them in 1 Peter 1. Here is Peter's take on them:

"For you have been born again, not of perishable seed, but of imperishable, through the living and enduring word of God.
For,
'All people are like grass,
    and all their glory is like the flowers of the field;
the grass withers and the flowers fall,
    but the word of the Lord endures for ever.'
And this is the word that was preached to you."

(1 Peter 1:23-25)

Peter's point is that what God does in us is enduring because his word is enduring. We have been born again with imperishable seed—imperishable DNA, we might say today—because that seed was planted in us through the imperishable word.

This is so encouraging. Maybe you think, "If only our meetings were as entertaining as those of big churches, or if only our presentations could match the latest music videos, or if only our pastor was as slick as TV presenters—then we'd get results." And it's true that if you can entertain, you may well draw a crowd. But this doesn't produce lasting growth. It's the enduring word that produces enduring results. Other approaches might produce quicker results. But "the grass withers and the flowers fall." Meanwhile, says Isaiah, "the word of our

God endures for ever" (Isaiah **40:8**). And, Peter says, the enduring word creates enduring people.

A God beyond compare

The big theme of Isaiah 40 – 55 is that the Lord will redeem his people and lead them home to demonstrate that he is beyond compare. He alone is enthroned above the earth, and the nations are as nothing before him. Throughout this section God repeatedly declares, "I am the LORD" (41:4, 13, 17; 42:6, 8; 43:1, 15; 44:24; 45:3, 5, 6, 7, 8, 18, 19, 21; 49:23, 26; 51:15). Seven times he also declares, "I am he" (41:4; 43:10; 46:4; 48:12) or "It is I" (52:6) or "I, even I, am he" (43:25; 51:12). This phrase echoes the I AM declaration to **Moses** at the burning bush in Exodus 3 and prefigures the "I am" sayings of Jesus in John's Gospel and Mark 6:50 and 14:62. Phrases about God creating things are also used repeatedly (Isaiah 43:1, 7, 15; 45:7, 8, 12, 18; 48:7; 54:16).

Isaiah expresses the supremacy of the LORD powerfully in 40:12-26, where he makes an explicit comparison between God and the nations. "Who has measured the waters in the hollow of his hand?" he asks (40:12). Who else but God! If you pour water into your hand, you can hold a spoonful or so of water in your palm. But God can hold whole oceans in the palm of his hand. Before God "the nations are like a drop in a bucket" (40:15). It's actually a drop *from* a bucket. If you empty out a bucket of water, you'll find there are a few drops left at the bottom. That's what the kings of the earth are like in comparison with God. Isaiah concludes, "Before him all the nations are as nothing; they are regarded by him as worthless and less than nothing" (40:17). God is on the throne, and therefore his people have no reason to complain, for God himself will renew their strength (40:27-31).

Having promised strength to his people in 40:29-31, God then calls on the nations to renew their strength so they are ready to participate in a court case with God (41:1). If the focus in chapter 40 was on God's sovereignty in *creation*, here it is on his sovereignty in *history* (41:2-4).

God then turns from the nations—leaving them to nail down their **idols** so they don't topple over (41:5-7)—to again strengthen the resolve of his people (41:8-10). God will give his people victory (41:11-20). Again and again his message is "Do not fear" (41:10, 13-14). Isaiah 41:14 says, "'Do not be afraid, you worm Jacob, little Israel, do not fear, for I myself will help you,' declares the LORD, your Redeemer, the Holy One of Israel." In chapters 1 – 39 the fact that the LORD is "the Holy One of Israel" was a reason for his discipline against unholy Israel. But now this name becomes the reason for his redemption, for the holy God will be true to his covenant commitments.

There is also a repeated emphasis on the fact that God alone knows the future (41:27; 43:9; 44:7; 46:10). God can *predict* the future because God *determines* the future (41:25). This ability to predict what is coming is a sign of his supremacy over rival claims (41:21-29). So the LORD is unique and eternal, and the Creator. "The LORD is the everlasting God, the Creator of the ends of the earth" (40:28). "I, the Lord—with the first of them and with the last—I am he" (41:4). "I am the first and I am the last; apart from me there is no God" (44:6). These descriptions of God are juxtaposed with descriptions of the futility of idols (42:17; 44:9-20; 45:16; 46:1, 5-7). Unlike God, idols cannot predict the future (42:8-9).

> "I am the LORD; that is my name!
> I will not yield my glory to another
> or my praise to idols." (42:8)

So Isaiah exhorts God's people to "sing to the LORD a new song" (42:10-12) for "the LORD will march out like a champion" to "triumph over his enemies" (42:13).

A servant who redeems

The other key focus of Isaiah 40 – 55 is on the Servant of the LORD, who is introduced in four "songs", the first of which is found in 42:1-9. The Servant is anointed by God's Spirit to bring justice to the nations (42:1-4). He will be "a light for the Gentiles" and "open eyes that are blind" (42:6-7).

Sometimes it seems that the Servant is Israel, while sometimes the Servant appears to be an individual who redeems Israel. Broadly speaking, in **40:1** – 44:23 the nation of Israel is God's Servant, for they were called to reveal God to the nations. But the people of Israel are blind and deaf (42:18-22; 43:8), just as God had said Isaiah would make them (6:9-10), because the people refuse to pay attention (42:23 – 25). So the nation cannot fulfil the role of God's Servant. Into this void steps King Cyrus (44:24 – 45:7), the foreign king who is nevertheless described as God's shepherd and anointed (literally his "messiah") (45:1). The task of Cyrus as God's servant is the immediate liberation of Judah from Babylonian exile. Finally, in 49:1-55:13 Isaiah promises an ultimate Servant, who will accomplish the ultimate liberation of all God's people through his own suffering and death (52:13 – 53:12). The Servant is a person who both embodies the **witness** of God's people and redeems them from their sin.

> Now, through Christ, the church is the servant of God, witnessing among the nations.

The New Testament applies the Servant songs of Isaiah both to Jesus and to the church. As we shall see, Jesus is both the light of the nations, who truly reveals God's glory, and the suffering Servant, who redeems God's people through his death. But in doing all this, he also renews the witness of his people. In Acts 13:47, for example, Paul applies this reference to the witness of the Servant in Isaiah 49:6 to the mission of himself and Barnabas. In other words, Israel was supposed to be God's witness but failed. But now, through Christ, the church is the servant of God, witnessing to him among the nations.

This brings us back to the opening words of this section. Consider the commands in **40:1-11**. We are told to "comfort" (**40:1**), "speak"

(**40:2**), "proclaim" (**40:2**), "cry out" (**40:6**), "lift up your voice" (**40:9**) and "say" (**40:9**). And then in **40:10** we're told to "see ... see." Not only that, but the main "characters" in this little drama are "a voice" (**40:3**), "a voice" (**40:6**) and "a voice" (**40:9**). We meet a voice calling in the wilderness (**40:3**), a voice telling Isaiah to "cry out" (**40:6**) and a voice proclaiming, "Here is your God!" (**40:9**) These "voices" represent God's people. The point is that God's people are a voice: we speak, we have something to say, we have good news to declare. So the application is clear: *lift up your voice.*

Questions for reflection

1. How do Isaiah 40:6-8 and 1 Peter 1:23-25 help you get the right perspective on evangelism?

2. Which of the images expressing God's supremacy do you find most compelling? What images of your own could you come up with?

3. How can you make being God's servant a priority? What will that look like in your life?

9. THE VICTORY OF GOD

FOCUS: ISAIAH 43

Do you like exams? Perhaps you can remember sitting in rows, waiting for someone to say, "You may turn over your papers and begin." Your future depended on how well you performed. We don't like being scrutinised. Perhaps you've worked for a boss who was always looking over your shoulder. Many workers in call centres are constantly being monitored. Or people in sales are ranked according to their performance. Or perhaps you've been on trial, standing in the dock, hearing the accusations against you read out, your future at stake. Some of us live life as if we're on trial. We never quite feel we belong. We worry about whether we really make the grade. In all sorts of situations we don't feel at home—perhaps even in the church. In Isaiah God promises to lead us home. He promises to bring us to a place of belonging and safety: a place where you can kick your shoes off and feel at home.

Isaiah's ministry took place when God's people were threatened by the Assyrian Empire. This is the dominant theme of chapters 1 – 39. But then, in the final verses of chapter 39, Isaiah predicts the defeat of Judah by the Babylonian Empire and their exile in Babylon around 120 years later in 587 BC. God's people are going to be examined, and they will fail the test. They will go away into exile. They will not feel at home because they will not be at home. But in chapters 40 – 66 Isaiah looks beyond this moment of judgment to offer hope. So these chapters speak to a situation two centuries *after* Isaiah's day.

Reader's guide

Isaiah 43

Isaiah promises a new exodus through which God will liberate his people from their captivity in Babylon. This points us forward to the liberation from sin and death that Jesus accomplishes. Just as the first exodus demonstrated the superiority of the LORD over the gods of Egypt, so this new exodus will demonstrate God's superiority over all other rivals (43:8-13).

Isaiah 44:1-23

God promises to renew his people (44:1-5). God mocks the folly of those who call on idols they have made to save them (44:6-20). People make an idol from dead wood and call it "my god". In 44:21-23 God says he has "made" Israel. False gods are dead images, but the true God has a living image in the form of his people.

Isaiah 44:24 - 45:25

God promises to defeat the Babylonian Empire through the Persian king, Cyrus. Only God can fulfil predictions of the future in this way because only he is "the LORD, the Maker of all things" (44:24-28). He describes Cyrus as "his anointed" (45:1). This is literally "his messiah". Even though Cyrus does not acknowledge God, God is going to use him to accomplish his purposes (45:4-5). All events are in God's hands, for he is the Creator (45:7-10). But again Isaiah looks beyond this immediate liberation to the greater liberation of Jesus. God's people will be saved "with an everlasting salvation" (45:17). Though God's ways are often hidden from us (45:15), what we need to do is clear (45:19). So the invitation goes out to all the earth: "Turn to me and be saved" (45:22).

Isaiah 46

The gods of Babylon (Bel and Nebo) are a burden to those who must carry them (46:1-2, 6-7). But God has carried his people (46:3-4). "I am God," says the LORD in 46:9-10, "and there is none like me. I make known the end from the beginning."

Isaiah 47

Isaiah personifies Babylon as a great queen (47:5). God used Babylon to chastise his people, but she failed to learn the very lessons she was dispensing (47:6-7). So she will fall in disgrace (47:1-3, 8-11). In contrast to God, the Babylonian astrologers cannot predict the future (47:12-15).

Isaiah 48

As God predicted, his people have repeatedly invoked his name without true faith (48:1-11). Now God predicts the defeat of Babylon through "the LORD's chosen ally"—that is, through King Cyrus (48:12-16). "I am the LORD your God," says 48:17, "who teaches you what is best for you". If God's people had "paid attention" to his commands, they would have enjoyed peace (48:18-22). Yet still, to display his grace, God will not destroy them completely (48:9-11).

Isaiah 43 contains many themes which run throughout chapters 40 – 48. God will reveal his glory and redeem his people through his Servant. What Isaiah 43 adds is the promise that God will redeem his people through a new exodus.

The new exodus

"I have redeemed you," says **43:1**. It's the language that was used of the exodus. God redeemed Israel from slavery in Egypt just as someone would have redeemed a slave from the slave market. He had led them out of Egypt through the waters of the Red Sea in Exodus 14 and into the promised land through the waters of the Jordan River in Joshua 3 – 4. Now he's going to do that again. That's what's described in Isaiah **43:2**:

> "When you pass through the waters,
>   I will be with you;
>   and when you pass through the rivers,
>   they will not sweep over you."

This is what happened at the Red Sea and the River Jordan, and this is what Isaiah says will happen again. God has redeemed his people at the expense of Egypt. The exodus was a choice *for* Israel and *against* Egypt. **43:3** puts it like this: "I give Egypt for your ransom, Cush [the upper Nile region] and Seba in your stead ... I will give people in exchange for you."

The exodus was also when Israel was first called God's son. God had said to Moses, "Then say to Pharaoh, 'This is what the LORD says: Israel is my firstborn son, and I told you, "Let my son go, so that he may worship me"'" (Exodus 4:22-23). Now in Isaiah **43:6** God speaks of "my sons ... and my daughters". Again, Isaiah is recalling the exodus. Except that Isaiah is not speaking of a past event in these verses. He's speaking of what God will do in the future. "I *will* be with you ... [the rivers] *will* not sweep over you ... you *will* not be burned ... I *will* give people in exchange for you ... I *will* ... gather you" (43:2-5). All the language is looking to the future.

Isaiah is looking *back* to the exodus as a precedent or, better still, a blueprint for what God will do in the *future*. Through a new exodus God's people will be gathered home to a new earth (4:5; 11:16; 40:1-11; 52; 61:6). Again and again, Isaiah speaks of a "highway" along which God will lead his people home (11:16; 19:23; 35:8; 49:11; 57:14).

When does this take place? In 44:24 – 45:25 God appoints Cyrus to "accomplish all that I please" (44:28; 45:1, 13; 48:14-15). Cyrus was the Persian king who, two centuries later, would defeat Babylon in 539 BC and allow the Jews to return to Judah. In 47:1-15 and 48:20-22 Isaiah proclaims the fall of Babylon. So Isaiah's words found a partial fulfilment 70 years after the Babylonian exile, when Ezra and Nehemiah led the Jews home. But that was only the beginning. In many ways the returning Jews still felt they were in exile. In Nehemiah 9:36 they speak of themselves as still being slaves because they're under the rule of foreign kings. This feeling persisted into the time of Jesus, when the Jews felt keenly their oppression by the Romans.

Notice, too, what it is *from which* God preserves his people: water and flames (Isaiah **43:2**). Deliverance from water was central to the first exodus, but not deliverance from flames. Yet we don't have to look far for a reference to flames. Chapter 42 ends with the flames of God's judgment licking around our feet. The LORD himself would hand over his people to exile, enveloping them in flames (42:24-25). Perhaps the water, too, echoes the judgment of God during Noah's flood. We are, as it were, surrounded by judgment. Then chapter 43 begins, "But now". Here's a glorious change of direction. In the first exodus God's people were delivered from Egypt. But this new exodus will deliver us from God's judgment.

Not only that, but Isaiah's description goes well beyond the return from Babylonian exile. If that was all he had in mind, then he would have just said, as he does in **43:6**, "I will say to the north, 'Give them up!'" The Babylonian Empire included lands to the north of Israel, and so that was the direction from which the exiles would return. But Isaiah says much more than this. God is going to gather his people from east and west, north and south, from the ends of the earth.

"I will bring your children from the east
   and gather you from the west.
I will say to the north, "Give them up!"
   and to the south, "Do not hold them back."
Bring my sons from afar
   and my daughters from the ends of the earth—
everyone who is called by my name." (**43:5-7**)

Jesus is the one who fulfils the promise of a new exodus. Indeed, by proclaiming God's promise of a new exodus, Isaiah was the crucial influence that enabled the writers of the New Testament to interpret what Jesus accomplished as the true exodus—the liberation from sin and death. As we saw when we looked at 40:3, Mark's Gospel begins with a quote from Isaiah 40 announcing the end of exile (Mark 1:3). In Isaiah 49:24-26 God promised to bind Babylon, the "strong man", to release his people, and in Mark 3:27 Jesus implies that he will bind Satan the "strong man". Jesus commands the sea just as God did during the exodus (Mark 4:39; 6:48-50). When his disciples were struggling in a storm, Jesus walked out to them on the water. Mark tells us, "He was about to pass by them." When they cried out in terror, Jesus said, "Take courage! It is I. Don't be afraid" (Mark 6:48-50). In other words, Jesus passed by on the sea to reveal "I am he"—just as the LORD passed by Moses in Exodus 34 and just as Isaiah reveals here in **43:10**. Like Moses on Mount Sinai, Jesus experiences glory on a mountain when he is **transfigured** (Exodus 24:12-16; 34:29-35; Mark 9:1-7). And, like Moses, Jesus descends from the mountain to find faithlessness (Exodus 32; Mark 9:14-19). The Passover meal transforms into a meal to celebrate our new exodus through Jesus our Passover Lamb (Mark 14:12-26). And that's just Mark's Gospel!

Throughout the New Testament the work of Jesus is described using exodus or new exodus language. In particular, the exodus model is behind the New Testament language of "redemption" (Romans 3:24; Colossians 1:13-14) and "inheritance" (1 Peter 1:3-5). At the transfiguration, Jesus, Moses and Elijah discuss "his departure"—it's literally "his exodus" (Luke 9:31). Jesus is "I am"—the Lord, who appeared to Moses in the burning bush (Exodus 3:14; John 8:58). He is the true Passover lamb, whose blood redeems us from sin and protects us from death (John 1:29; 1 Corinthians 5:7; 1 Peter 1:18-19). Luke's account of the Last Supper is full of references to the Passover, because Jesus is the true Passover lamb (Luke 22:1-20). As with the Passover lamb, his bones are not broken (Exodus 12:46; John 19:36).

> Isaiah promises a bigger, better exodus from slavery and death.

Just as the Israelites left Egypt without yeast (Exodus 12:17-20), so we're to leave behind our old way of life (1 Corinthians 5:6-8). Just as the Israelites passed through the waters of the Red Sea to a new life, so we pass through the waters of baptism (1 Corinthians 10:1-2).

Jesus is the true manna from heaven (John 6:31-35) and the true water from the rock (1 Corinthians 10:3-4). John says the Word "made his dwelling among us"—literally "tabernacled" among us (John 1:14). All these references are like hypertext links that take you to the story of the exodus. The New Testament portrays Jesus as the Redeemer, who sets us free and leads us home to God.

In this way Isaiah is a bridge between Exodus and the New Testament. He takes the language of the old exodus from Egypt and uses it to promise a bigger, better exodus from slavery and death. And Jesus is the ultimate fulfilment of Isaiah's promise.

Isaiah is also describing the mission of the church. Through the mission of the church God is gathering his people from the ends of the earth. He is leading us home to God, just as he led Israel through the wilderness. He is giving us an inheritance in the new creation, just as he gave Israel an inheritance in the promised land. This is the new exodus promised by Isaiah, and it's happening all around us. We ourselves are the evidence that this promise is being fulfilled.

Isaiah **43:1-7** is topped and tailed by Isaiah describing God as "he who created you ... he who formed you" and God describing Israel as those "whom I created ... whom I formed" (**43:1, 7**; see also 45:18-19). This is not a reference to the creation of the world but to the creation of Israel as God's people through the exodus (Hosea 11:1-4). For Isaiah, God's people were Israel and Judah. In the **new covenant** God's people are the church—you and me. We are the people he formed, redeemed and summoned.

What's striking about this language is how intimate it is. Maybe you feel like you're sinking or being overwhelmed by life. Or maybe you're feeling the heat. God says to you today through Isaiah:

"When you pass through the waters,
    I will be with you ...
When you walk through the fire,
    you will not be burned ...
You are precious and honoured in my sight,

and … I love you …

[so] do not be afraid, for I am with you." (**43:2-5**)

God on trial

The language of "gathering" continues in the next section (**43:8-13**). But this gathering is very different. Here God is summoning the nations for a court case:

"All the nations gather together
    and the peoples assemble.
Which of their gods foretold this
    and proclaimed to us the former things?
Let them bring in their witnesses to prove they were right,
    so that others may hear and say, 'It is true.'
'You are my witnesses,' declares the LORD,
    'and my servant whom I have chosen,
so that you may know and believe me
    and understand that I am he.'" (**43:9-10**; see also 45:20-25)

It's God who is on trial. Or rather God is the plaintiff. Today in criminal court cases we have one defendant who is prosecuted by the state. But in Hebrew courts there was no state prosecutor. One person brought an accusation against another. So in effect two people were on trial. The trial would inevitably end with one person being vindicated and the other being condemned. In this trial the LORD brings his accusation against the other gods of the world. And this trial will end with one party being vindicated and the other being condemned.

The new exodus puts God to the test—just as the first exodus did. During the first exodus God told Pharaoh, "I have raised you up for this very purpose, that I might show you my power and that my name might be proclaimed in all the earth" (Exodus 9:16). The first exodus was a contest between the gods of Egypt and the God of Israel. The new exodus is no different. At stake is this: Who is the true God? Who is worth following?

God's claim is that other gods are imposters and that he alone is God. He puts his case in Isaiah **43:9**: "Which of their gods foretold this and proclaimed to us the former things?" In Isaiah 40 – 48 God is predicting what will happen ahead of time. As we have seen, in 44:28 and 45:1 and 13 he speaks of the Persian king, Cyrus, naming him two centuries before he was even a twinkle in his parents' eyes! God's ability to speak of the future is presented again and again in these chapters as proof of his uniqueness compared with other so-called gods (41:21-29; 42:8-9; 44:7; 45:14, 20-21; 46:10). God is the true God because he can predict the future, and he can predict the future because he determines the future.

Questions for reflection

1. Who do you know who especially needs to hear the message that God is with them and has promised a home for them?

2. How does reflecting on stories of what God has done help you to keep on following God in the present?

3. Are you ever tempted to think that it's not worth sharing the good news of Jesus with people of other faiths? How does this passage challenge you? How might you gently show them that their gods are not the true God?

PART TWO

God summons the nations to a court case. At stake is whether the LORD is the true God or whether the idols of the nations are. Here's the evidence for the LORD:

"'Before me no god was formed,
    nor will there be one after me.
I, even I, am the LORD,
    and apart from me there is no saviour.
I have revealed and saved and proclaimed—
    I, and not some foreign god among you.
You are my witnesses,' declares the LORD, 'that I am God.
    Yes, and from ancient days I am he.
No one can deliver out of my hand.
    When I act, who can reverse it?'" (**43:10-13**)

Imagine a product comparison website. Each option has a list of specifications lined up so we can compare products. God is inviting just such a comparison here. When we compare God with any other gods or ideologies, what do we see? What's the evidence?

1. *The LORD is the Creator.* "Before me no god was formed" (**43:10**). He is the Creator (45:9-12; 48:12-13). All other gods are themselves creations. In 44:6-20 and 46:1-7 Isaiah ruthlessly mocks the worship of idols created by human beings (see also 45:15-17).

2. *The LORD is the Saviour.* "Apart from me there is no saviour" (**43:11**). That's why we are God's witnesses. We are the living proof that God, and God alone, can save. "I, and not some foreign god," saved you (**43:12**). Perhaps God has in mind the golden calf. The people worshipped the **golden calf**, saying, "These are your gods, Israel, who brought you up out of Egypt" (Exodus 32:4). But in reality it was the LORD who had saved them.

3. *The LORD is the Revealer.* "I have revealed and ... proclaimed" (Isaiah **43:12**). God has spoken through his prophets, through his

Son and in his word. Only God can speak of the future (**43:9**; 41:21-29; 42:8-9; 44:7; 45:21; 46:10; 48:16).

4. *The LORD is the sovereign King.* "No one can deliver out of my hand. When I act, who can reverse it?" (**43:13**) No god can undo the work of God.

This is why the message goes to the ends of the earth: because the LORD alone is the Creator, Saviour, Revealer and King. No one else can create, recreate, save, reveal and reign (see also 45:2-8, 14). God himself declares:

"Turn to me and be saved,
　all you ends of the earth;
　for I am God, and there is no other." (45:22)

But the most extraordinary thing about this trial is that the cry goes out, *Call the first witness,* and it's *you* who is being summoned! In **43:9** God invites the nations to bring their witnesses. The nations will speak on behalf of their gods. Meanwhile the witnesses for God's defence are God's people. "'You are my witnesses,' declares the LORD," in **43:10** and **12**. God is on trial, history is the courtroom and God's people are the defence witnesses.

The problem is that humanity is the judge, and humanity is blind and deaf (**43:8**). Let's go back to our product comparison website. The "spec" list is lined up, each product side by side. But humanity refuses to follow the evidence. So in the end what decides the matter will be the customer reviews—what you and I tell people about our experience of God. Isaiah is describing the mission of the church. Our role is to testify to God before humanity. *You*—in your daily life, in the testimony you give, in the "review" of God you provide—*you are God's defence witness.*

What's at stake is people's confidence in God to save. When Judah is defeated by Babylon, many will doubt the LORD's ability to save. Many will wonder whether the Babylonian gods are in fact more powerful. Maybe you wonder the same as Islam grows stronger or the new atheists pour scorn on Christianity or church attendance decreases or people explain faith in purely psychological terms. Who is powerful to save? When you face redundancy or you're hit by depression or you feel lonely or Satan accuses you or your church faces closure or you hide a secret sin—then you need to put your faith in the one who declares:

> "I have revealed and saved and proclaimed—
>> I, and not some foreign god among you …
> No one can deliver out of my hand.
>> When I act, who can reverse it?" (**43:12-13**)

In other words, *I have done what no other god can do. And what I have done no other god can undo.*

The new exodus again

Isaiah tells the story a second time. In **43:1-7** Isaiah spoke of a new exodus, and he does so again in **43:14-21**. Like the opening verses, these verses begin, "This is what the LORD says". And, like **43:1**, they begin with a reference to God as our Redeemer (**43:14**).

God is also described as "the Holy One of Israel". In chapters 1 – 39 this description of God was used to signal his judgment: mess with the Holy One and you will end up worse off. But here the description of God as "the Holy One of Israel" forms the basis for hope.

> "This is what the LORD says—
>> he who made a way through the sea,
>> a path through the mighty waters,
> who drew out the chariots and horses,
>> the army and reinforcements together,
> and they lay there, never to rise again,
>> extinguished, snuffed out like a wick." (**43:16-17**)

It's a description of the parting of the Red Sea. God made a way through the sea and led Israel to safety. Then, when the Egyptian army tried to follow them, the army was extinguished. Isaiah **43:20** continues, "I provide water in the wilderness and streams in the wasteland, to give drink to my people". It's an allusion to Exodus 15 and 17, when God healed bitter water and provided water from a rock. God is going to do it again as he brings his people out of Babylon (Isaiah **43:14**). But God goes further in **43:18-19**:

"Forget the former things;
   do not dwell on the past.
See, I am doing a new thing!"

It's as if God is saying, *Never mind the exodus from Egypt; I'm going to do something new, something bigger, something better. The first exodus was impressive; but the coming exodus is going to be off the scale.*

- We are freed—not from Egypt but from the tyranny of sin.

- We escape—not physical death on Passover night but eternal death.

- We are led—not to the promised land but to a home in the renewed creation.

- We are fed—not with **manna**, but with Jesus himself.

Humanity on trial

So exodus is what God has done, and new exodus is what God will do—and what God has *now* done through Jesus. But look at **43:22**: "Yet you have not called on me, Jacob, you have not wearied yourselves for me, Israel". The people of Judah can't even be bothered to ask for God's help. It's not that God's demands are a burden. "I have not burdened you with **grain offerings**," says God in **43:23**, "nor wearied you with demands for incense". But in contrast **43:24** says, "But you have burdened me with your sins and wearied me with your offences." It's the people's actions which are burdensome. In 48:1-11 God says he has foretold the future so that Israel will learn to trust him, for he knows how "stubborn" and "treacherous" they are (48:4, 8, 17-19).

So God calls another trial. And this time it's *humanity* which is in the dock. This is what happened at the first exodus. The need for water in the desert "put them to the test" (Exodus 15:25). In Exodus 17:1-7 a trial was convened, and now the trial is reconvened. "Review the past for me," says God in Isaiah **43:26**, "let us argue the matter together; state the case for your innocence". But there is no case for our innocence. "Your first father sinned," says **43:27**. Adam rebelled against God, and everything has unravelled since then. And so the verdict is "destruction" (**43:28**).

But look at **43:25**:

"I, even I, am he who blots out
   your transgressions, for my own sake,
   and remembers your sins no more."

For God's people this trial has a twist, and the twist is *Jesus*. Central to the first exodus was Passover. As God prepared to come in judgment on Egypt, God's people sacrificed a lamb and daubed its blood around their doors. God killed every firstborn child in Egypt except where the blood was daubed. The lamb died in the place of the child. God's people escaped slavery and death through the Passover lamb. 800 years after Isaiah, John the Baptist saw Jesus and said, "Look, the Lamb of God, who takes away the sin of the world!" (John 1:29; see also 1 Peter 1:18-19) The trial is called. The evidence is presented. The verdict is clear. But Jesus steps in and takes our place. The judgment falls on our Passover lamb. As a result, God "blots out your transgressions ... and remembers your sins no more" (Isaiah **43:25**).

There will be a final day of judgment, but for us the trial is done and dusted.

All the scrutiny is done. It's true that there will be a final day of judgment, but for us the trial is over. It was done and dusted with the death and resurrection of Jesus. "He was delivered over to death for our sins," says Romans 4:25, "and was raised to life for our **justification**". The "not guilty" verdict has already been delivered.

The examination is over, and you have passed with full marks because you get the grade that Jesus deserves.

Why does God do this? In Isaiah **43:25** God says, "For my own sake" (see also 48:9, 11). God sent Jesus as a Passover lamb for our sake: that is, to meet your need. But he also sent Jesus for *his* sake: that is, to reveal his glory and grace. "God raised us up with Christ and seated us with him in the heavenly realms in Christ Jesus," says Ephesians 2:6-7, "in order that in the coming ages he might show the incomparable riches of his grace, expressed in his kindness to us in Christ Jesus". Throughout all eternity we will be "to the praise of his glorious grace" (Ephesians 1:6).

Finally, notice how God continues in Isaiah 44:1-3:

"But now listen, Jacob, my servant,
    Israel, whom I have chosen.
This is what the LORD says—
    he who made you, who formed you in the womb,
    and who will help you:
do not be afraid, Jacob, my servant,
    Jeshurun, whom I have chosen.
For I will pour water on the thirsty land,
    and streams on the dry ground;
I will pour out my Spirit on your offspring,
    and my blessing on your descendants."

Here is God promising to lead his people home. The words echo **43:19-21**. Here, again, is an echo of Exodus 15 and 17, when God provided water in the wilderness for Israel. God will protect his people (from wild animals) and provide for his people (with water in the desert) on their journey through life. He will ensure we make it home to glory. Here is the evidence and fruit of the forgiveness of sin that he promises in Isaiah **43:25**.

But notice *how* God protects and provides for his people: "I will pour out my Spirit on your offspring" (44:3). Jesus reiterates this promise in John 7:37-39, where he promises living water flowing from within to all who come to him. John adds that Jesus meant by this the gift of the Spirit. In other words, this promise finds its fulfilment on the Day of Pentecost. It is the Spirit who leads us and guides us—just as Israel was led by the pillars of cloud and fire (Exodus 13:21-22). The Spirit leads us from slavery to sonship (Romans 8:14-15). Just as the Spirit of God accompanied and guided God's people through the wilderness on their way to the promised land, so today the Spirit of God accompanies and guides us as we take the message of Christ to the ends of the earth. We are not alone, for God is present *among* us and *within* us.

So Jesus leads us home through a new exodus. In the future he will lead us to a new home in a new heaven and a new earth—more of that in Isaiah 65. But already he has led us home to God. We can feel at home in God's presence, for there is no condemnation. God promises not to remember your sins any more (**43:25**). Don't be better at remembering your sin than God is! If you're in Christ by faith, you can say, "I belong to the LORD" (44:5). You belong in God's family, in God's presence, in God's future. You can kick your shoes off, put your feet on the sofa and feel at home.

Questions for reflection

1. What helps you to put your confidence in God's power to save?

2. What aspect of the story of exodus do you find most helpful for understanding what Jesus came to do?

3. How does it feel to say, "I belong to the LORD"? What difference might that make to your thinking and the way you treat others?

10. THE SUFFERING OF GOD'S SERVANT

FOCUS: ISAIAH 49

"What's it worth?" One way or another that's a question we often ask. You ask someone to do something and the reply comes, "What's it worth?" *How are you going to value my time?*

In the UK television programme *Antiques Roadshow,* people take what they hope are valuable antiques to be evaluated by experts. The experts pad it out, but the moment we're waiting for is when they announce an item's value. We love it when it turns out to be worth far more than anyone imagined. A few years ago they had a painting by the 17th-century artist Anthony van Dyck, which the owner had bought for £400 ($560) but which was valued by the show's experts at £400,000 ($560,000).

Imagine you could bring the cross of Christ to the experts on the *Antiques Roadshow*. What would they make of it? What value would they attach to it? In Isaiah 49 we discover what the cross of Jesus is worth.

We're introduced in **49:1** to the servant of the LORD. God calls him "my servant" in **49:3**. In **49:5** the Servant says the LORD "formed me in the womb to be his servant". Indeed, these verses are a conversation between the Servant and the LORD.

Reader's guide

Isaiah 49

In 49:1-7 we listen in to a dialogue between the LORD and his servant. God will reward the servant by giving him people from every nation through a new exodus (49:8-13). God has not forgotten his people (49:14-16). He will gather his children home in triumph to an enlarged land (49:17-26).

Isaiah 50

The reason for the exile was not that God is weak (50:2-3) but because of Judah's sin (50:1, 10-11). In contrast to the nation, the Servant (who is ultimately Jesus) has faithfully conveyed the message given to him by the LORD, even though doing so has meant abuse and mockery (50:4-9).

Isaiah 51:1-16

*In 51:1 Isaiah calls on God's people to "look to the rock from which you were cut". In other words, they're to remember Abraham—the father of the nations—and remember how God has faithfully fulfilled his promise to Abraham (51:2-3). God's salvation "will last for ever" (51:4-8) because the ancient monsters (**Rahab**, also Leviathan) of the primordial chaos—a picture perhaps of Satan and his angels—will be defeated (51:9-16; see also 27:1).*

Isaiah 51:17 - 52:12

Twice Isaiah calls on God's people to "awake" (51:17 and 52:1). Judah has "drunk from the hand of the LORD the cup of his wrath"—a picture of receiving God's judgment (51:17-20). But now God is going to take this cup away from his people (51:21-23). This was partially fulfilled when the Jews had spent 70 years in captivity in Babylon. But it was ultimately fulfilled when Jesus took God's judgment in our place (Mark 10:38). So God's people will be able to awake from their captivity (Isaiah 52:1-6, 11-12). In 52:7-10 we are told that to proclaim salvation is a beautiful thing to do: "How beautiful on the mountains are the feet of those who bring good news, who proclaim peace, who bring good tidings, who proclaim salvation" (52:7). Paul quotes this verse in Romans 10:15 to show that it has always been God's intention for "all the ends of the earth [to] see the salvation of our God" (Isaiah 52:10).

But who is this Servant? **49:3** clearly says that the servant is the nation of Israel: "[The LORD] said to me, 'You are my servant, Israel, in whom I will display my splendour'". **Verse 6** says the Servant is "a light for the Gentiles" or "nations". That's the kind of language that was used of Israel. They were to live under God's rule expressed in the law in such a way that the nations would see that it is good to know God (Deuteronomy 4:5-8). Isaiah himself uses this kind of language in Isaiah 2:2-5: "Come, descendants of Jacob, let us walk in the light of the LORD." Why? So that "many peoples will come and say, 'Come, let us go up to the mountain of the LORD'". The people of Israel were to attract the nations to God. So the Servant is Israel.

And yet Isaiah here was looking forward to a time when Israel would be in exile in Babylon. Instead of attracting the nations to the ways of the LORD, Israel had been attracted to the ways of the nations. Instead of honouring his name among the nations, she had **profaned** his name. *Be holy for I am holy* was the refrain of the law of Moses (Leviticus 11:44-45; 19:2; 20:26; Deuteronomy 23:14). In rescuing Israel from Egypt, God had linked his name with his people, and Israel was therefore obligated to honour God's name in their corporate life. But Israel was anything but holy. One of Isaiah's favourite ways of referring to God was "the holy one of Israel". But God had become the holy one of *unholy* Israel. God's reputation was on the line. The result was exile. Israel were judged for their sin. All those years spent conquering the land, creating a dynasty and building a temple had come to nothing. "I have laboured in vain," says the Servant in **49:4**, "I have spent my strength for nothing at all". The land lies desolate, the king is a captive and the temple is in ruins. Israel has failed to be the servant of the LORD.

But this is not the end of the story. In **49:5** the Servant is someone *other* than Israel, because *he* is going to gather Israel back to God: "And now the LORD says—he who formed me in the womb to be his servant to bring Jacob back to him and gather Israel to himself…" A new Servant, a true Servant, is going to redeem and restore Israel. More than this, the LORD says, "I will also make you a light for the Gentiles" (**49:6**). In other words, the coming Servant would be the light of the world that Israel was supposed to have been.

The Servant is honoured

A few hundred years later, the Lord Jesus stood up and declared, "I am the light of the world" (John 8:12). Jesus is the promised true and faithful Servant. (We'll return to this theme of light to the nations when we look at Isaiah 60.) What makes Jesus different? In **49:3** the LORD says, "You are my servant, Israel, in whom I will display my splendour," and Jesus perfectly displays the splendour of God. "The Son," says Hebrews 1:3, "is the radiance of God's glory and the exact representation of his being". If you want to know what God is like, look at Jesus. It's in Jesus that we see the true holiness, grace, wisdom, justice, compassion, power and love of God. And what we see is splendid, for he displays God's splendour. God's honour has been brought into question by the defeat of his people (Isaiah 52:3-6), but the Servant will restore God's reputation.

But what is the Servant worth? What reward does his obedience merit? Isaiah **49:5b** says, "For I am honoured in the eyes of the LORD". God is going to vindicate his Servant (50:7-11). God is going to reward the obedience of Jesus. God is going to give him what he's worth. And what is that reward? His people Israel. Isaiah is writing to Israel in exile under God's judgment. But God promises to restore them and return them to the land.

But—and this is the key point in Isaiah 49—that is not enough. The obedience of Christ is worth more. The cross of Christ is worth more. In **49:6** the LORD says, "It is too small a thing for you to be my servant to restore the tribes of Jacob and bring back those of Israel I have kept". It is too small a thing for Jesus to restore Israel. The cross deserves more and achieves more. So God says, "I will also make you a light for the Gentiles, that my salvation may reach to the ends of the earth".

Jesus left the glory of heaven. He did not cling to the rights of his divinity. He took on human form. He became, says Philippians 2:7, a servant—the Servant promised by Isaiah. He was obedient to death, even death on a cross. The judgment of exile was focused down on Jesus. He died under the darkness of judgment, forsaken by his Father. What is that worth? It is worth the nations! Not one nation. Not two or three nations. People from every nation—people from the ends of the earth. That's why we go to the nations in mission. Israel is not enough; Britain is not enough; the United States is not enough. Jesus deserves the praise of every nation.

> Why do we go in mission? To gather the nations to worship.

In **49:4** the Servant says, "What is due to me is in the LORD's hand". It's the language of the law court. It is literally "My judgment is in the LORD's hand". On earth Jesus was tried by humanity and found guilty. He was condemned as a blasphemer and executed as a rebel. But that decision has been overturned in the court of heaven. The ascension of Jesus is previewed by the vision in Daniel 7, where what Daniel saw was a courtroom. Jesus ascended through the clouds to be vindicated by the Ancient of Days. And what did he receive from the Ancient of Days? The nations. Daniel 7:14 says, "He was given authority, glory and sovereign power; all nations and peoples of every language worshipped him". Jesus echoes these words in the **Great Commission**: "All authority in heaven and on earth has been given to me. Therefore go and make disciples of all nations" (Matthew 28:18-19). Why do we go in mission? To gather the nations to worship Jesus.

The vindication of Jesus has already happened in heaven. And one day it will be matched on earth. Every knee will bow before him and every tongue acknowledge that he is Lord (Philippians 2:10-11). But the vindication of Jesus is also anticipated...

- every time we sing—as we gather to extol his praises.

- every time we sacrifice—as we display his worth through what we give up for him.

- every time we speak—since Isaiah **49:2** suggests that the Servant reigns through his word; therefore we extend that reign as we speak his word.

- every time someone is saved—as people are gathered from the nations to join us in worshipping Jesus.

Every step we make in mission is a step towards the moment when people from every nation, tribe, language and tongue join together to cry, "Worthy is the Lamb, who was slain, to receive power and wealth and wisdom and strength and honour and glory and praise!" (Revelation 5:12).

It is too small a thing to be concerned just for your family or parish. Christ is worth more than that. The cross of Christ deserves the nations.

I cannot tell how silently he suffered,
As with his peace he graced this place of tears,
Or how his heart upon the cross was broken,
The crown of pain to three and thirty years ...
But this I know, all flesh shall see his glory,
And he shall reap the harvest he has sown,
And some glad day his sun shall shine in splendour
When he the Saviour, Saviour of the world, is known.

(William Y. Fullerton, 1929)

The hymn continues, "I cannot tell how all the lands shall worship". In other words, I cannot tell how the progress of mission will unfold. I cannot tell how God will use any one of us to bring the gospel to the nations—how he might lead you or surprise you; whether you will see much fruit or little; whether you will suffer.

But this I know, the skies will thrill with rapture,
And myriad, myriad human voices sing,
And earth to heaven, and heaven to earth, will answer:
At last the Saviour, Saviour of the world, is King!

Questions for reflection

1. What is the cross worth to you? How can you express its worth in your life?

2. Does it surprise you that you are part of Jesus' reward for his obedience? How does that change your view of yourself?

3. Does this passage change the way you think about church missions? What will you do in response?

PART TWO

The first part of Isaiah 49 establishes that the obedience of the Servant Jesus merits the nations as a reward. The rest of the chapter describes *how* Jesus will receive his reward. As Isaiah so often does, it promises a new exodus. God is going to hear the cries of his people and re-member his covenant (**49:8**), just as he did at the first exodus (Exodus 2:23-25). God is going "to say to the captives, 'Come out,' and to those in darkness, 'Be free!'" (Isaiah **49:9**; 52:2). He's going to protect his people as they come home through the wilderness (**49:10**). "I will turn all my mountains into roads" (**49:11**). In other words, everyone will be coming home, out of exile, back to God (see also 51:10-11, 14-15; 52:11-12).

The Servant's children

But the covenant expands as it is renewed in Jesus (**49:8**). It is not enough to restore the tribes of Jacob. In Christ salvation reaches to the ends of the earth. So the new exodus is the promise of a new humanity made up of people from every nation. This whole chapter is addressed to the "islands", which is Isaiah's way of talking about the Gentiles (**49:1**). **49:12** says, "See, they will come from afar—some from the north, some from the west, some from the region of As-wan". Aswan is in the south of Egypt. Isaiah doesn't know the name of anywhere further away than that! God's people are going to be gathered from the four corners of the earth. So Isaiah is not just talk-ing about the Jews coming back home to Judah from bondage in Babylon; he's talking about people from every nation coming back home to God from bondage to sin. The new exodus will be so radical that it will lead to a new creation.

These words—words spoken 27 centuries ago—are being fulfilled today in the mission of the church, in a thousand stories of God hav-ing compassion on people and leading them home through Christ.

These words are being fulfilled as you send, give, pray and go to gather the nations.

With this in mind, the remainder of Isaiah 49 is a promise to us as we engage in mission. Throughout the second half of the chapter, Isaiah repeatedly uses the word "children" (**49:15, 17, 20, 22** and **25**; in **49:22** the NIV translates it "sons" because it is used alongside "daughters"). As we have seen, Isaiah is speaking to God's people in exile with their children far from home. For Isaiah's readers in Babylon, that meant the prospect of their children heading home to a renewed homeland—a powerfully evocative idea for any refugee. But Isaiah is looking beyond exile in Babylon to the work of Christ and the mission of the church. So "your children" are God's people, perhaps especially God's people waiting to be gathered into Christ's kingdom—waiting to become God's children in response to the proclamation of the gospel.

1. The LORD will remember his children

For many years I faithfully collected my daughters from school. Each day I walked up to the school to collect them. On one occasion I was so engrossed in my work that I forgot. Just one occasion! But whenever there is any discussion of parenting in our house, this one time gets dragged up again. My daughters delight in telling everyone what a terrible parent I was because I abandoned them in the school playground. All the hundreds of times I remembered are ignored.

The people complain, "The LORD has forsaken me, the Lord has forgotten me" (**49:14**). Parents don't normally forget their children. But it can happen, as we have noted. But not with God: God never forgets. The LORD continues:

"Can a mother forget the baby at her breast
    and have no compassion on the child she has borne?
Though she may forget,
    I will not forget you!

See, I have engraved you on the palms of my hands;
your walls are ever before me." (**49:15-16**)

When Isaiah writes those words, they're simply a graphic image of God's commitment to his people—like people who write reminders to themselves on their hands in pen. It's as if God has tattooed our names on his hands. But these words have added power for us because God's commitment to us is written in the scars on the palms of Jesus. He can never forget his people.

> God's commitment to us is written in scars on the palms of Jesus.

The point is that not one of God's people gets forgotten. "Your children hasten back," says **49:17-18**, "and those who laid you waste depart from you. Lift up your eyes and look around; all your children gather and come to you." We don't have to convert people. God's chosen people will respond when they hear the gospel. All we do is proclaim the message, and the harvest is guaranteed. None of God's chosen people gets left behind.

2. The LORD will multiply his children

Imagine waking up one day and finding you have a house full of children and they are complaining that the house is too small! "Where have they all come from?!" you say. "I'm sure I would have remembered if I'd given birth to dozens of children." In the same way, the people of Israel will look at the people of God and say, "I don't remember giving birth to all these children!" But, of course, these children are not all ethnic Jews. The nations have come and joined God's people. They have swelled the number beyond measure.

In **49:6** what was too small was the reward of the Servant. So now the nations are coming, and the numbers are growing. As a result, in **49:19-20** what is too small is the place for us all to live in. "This place is too small for us," the people say; "give us more space to live in". It's as if we're all crammed into Palestine and people are saying, *This place is never going to be big enough. We need a new heaven and a new earth.* And soon Isaiah will say, *It's coming* (65:17).

The church in the West feels small. Numbers are declining. We see few conversions. Churches are closing. But remember, this is just one place, and this is just one moment in history. A day is coming when we will say, as the people do in **49:21**, "I was left all alone, but these— where have they come from?"

At the moment we feel how alone we are. But one day we will say, "Where have they all come from?" We will stand around the throne of the Lamb, and we will see people stretching as far as the eye can see. There will be more people than there is sand on the seashore. And we will say, "Where have they have all come from?" And then maybe we will say, "Worthy is the Lamb. This is the reward that Christ deserves."

3. The LORD will vindicate his children

Isaiah promises that one day the people of this world will "bow down" before the people of God (**49:7, 22-23**). Having tasted the judgment of God (51:17-20), Jerusalem can now clothe herself with strength and splendour (52:1). "Kings will be your foster fathers, and their queens your nursing mothers" (**49:23**). We rarely think of governments and authorities nurturing the church! At the moment in the West, Christianity is marginalised. Fifty years ago a biblical **worldview** was part of the mainstream, but now we're on the margins. More than that, in the last ten years a biblical worldview has come to be seen as deviant. Our views on the sanctity of life, sex within marriage, and the reality of hell are now seen not just as wrong but as deviant and embarrassing.

Elsewhere in the world things are much tougher. In North Korea, Afghanistan and Pakistan the church faces intense persecution with Christians placed in labour camps or left unprotected from mob violence. There are an estimated 60,000 believers in the brutal prison camps of North Korea. Yet the church in North Korea is growing. North Koreans are fleeing to neighbouring countries in search of food, coming to Christ *and* choosing to go back to share their faith. Lisa Pearce, CEO of Open Doors UK, comments, "They see the beauty and worth of Jesus more clearly than we do, and they are finding him faithful" (Lisa Pearce, 'Letter from Lisa: Wake Up!' *Open Doors Magazine*, January 2018, p 3). At the moment it's tough. But it will be worth it. One day God's people will be vindicated, and it will be clear that Christ is worth it. "Those who hope in me will not be disappointed" (**49:23**).

4. The LORD will liberate his children

"Can plunder be taken from warriors, or captives be rescued from the fierce?" asks Isaiah in **49:24**. We look around us, and we feel the power of Satan. "The god of this age," says Paul, "has blinded the minds of unbelievers, so that they cannot see the light of the gospel that displays the glory of Christ" (2 Corinthians 4:4). And so we can wonder how anyone will ever see Christ's glory. Perhaps there are people in your family or among your friends who you can't imagine being converted—people whose lives are so troubled, or whose hearts are so hardened, or who've rejected the gospel so many times. Can they be rescued from the grip of Satan?

God responds in Isaiah **49:25**:

"Yes, captives will be taken from warriors,
   and plunder retrieved from the fierce;
I will contend with those who contend with you,
   and your children I will save."

Through the cross and resurrection, Satan has been bound so that his power is limited (Mark 3:23-27; Luke 10:18; Revelation 12:7-9; 20:1-6). God is in the business of rescuing people from the dominion of darkness and bringing them into the kingdom of the Son he loves (Colossians 1:13).

For over 25 years I've prayed for my wider family. I long ago ran out of ways of varying my prayers. I couldn't imagine how God would save them. Yet recently my niece was saved through a church toddler group. I don't know whether individuals in your family or among your friends will be saved. But I know this: Christ will have his reward. We should expect unbelievers to have their eyes opened, their hearts melted and their lives changed. And we should expect believers to endure hardship, resist temptation and serve Christ. For God's children are being wrenched from the grip of Satan. That is what the cross achieved, and that is what the cross deserves.

What's it worth? What's the cross worth to you? Enough to give? To send? To pray? To go? God thinks the cross is worth the nations. What do you think it's worth?

Questions for reflection

1. What is your experience of parenting? How is God a better parent?

2. What, if anything, causes you to despair for the future of the church? How does this passage address those feelings?

3. Who will you pray for as a result of reading this chapter?

11. THE JUDGMENT OF GOD'S SERVANT

FOCUS: ISAIAH 52:13 - 53:12

Isaiah 53 is perhaps the famous passage in the book of Isaiah and one of the most famous passages in the entire Old Testament. It's the fourth and final Servant song. Israel, as we have seen, had failed to be a faithful servant of God. So Isaiah promised a coming Servant who would redeem God's people and become the light to the nations which Israel had failed to be. This promise is, as we have also seen, a promise fulfilled in Jesus. Here in Isaiah 53 we discover how Jesus will redeem his people.

Reader's guide

Isaiah 52:13 - 53:12

The Servant of the LORD (who is Jesus) suffers the punishment of God on behalf of God's people and so justifies many.

Isaiah 54

As a result of the suffering and triumph of Jesus the Servant, many people are going to be saved. Like a once-barren woman bearing many children, God's fruitless people are going to see many converts (54:1). So the call goes out to "enlarge the place of your tent" (54:2-3). We are going to need a big building project to accommodate the many people flooding in from the nations.

- God's people will expand (54:1-3).
- God's people will forget their shame (54:4-8).
- God's people will never again be judged (54:9-10).
- God's people will be secure (54:11-17).

Isaiah 55

In chapter 55 the invitation to enjoy the fruit of the Servant's triumph goes out. Isaiah calls us to turn from our empty, unsatisfying ways and find true satisfaction in God (55:1-7). This is the call that comes to us today in the gospel. God's word is going to reap a harvest (55:8-11). Even the created world will be caught up in the redemption of humanity (55:12-13; Romans 8:19-21).

Contempt

This song is in five stanzas or sections, each made up of three Bible verses. The first stanza in Isaiah **52:13-15** contains hints of the climax of the song, to which we will return. But its main theme, along with the second stanza (**53:1-3**), is the contempt in which the Servant of the LORD is held by humanity. "Many ... were appalled at him," says **52:14**. It continues:

"His appearance was so disfigured beyond that of any human being and his form marred beyond human likeness." (**52:14**)

Think of Jesus hanging on the cross. The whips with which he was scourged have pulled away his flesh until his bone is exposed. The crown of thorns has sent trickles of blood down his face. His weakened frame has collapsed under the weight of the cross. Now the nails hold his body in an unnatural, twisted shape. His face is harrowed by the inner anguish of his soul. As a result, he looks less than human—his humanity has been stripped from him. "Who has believed our message?" asks **53:1**. Jesus has claimed to be the Son of God, the Saviour of the world, and the promised Messiah. But those claims seem sheer madness as he hangs on the cross.

"He had no beauty or majesty to attract us to him," says **53:2**, "nothing in his appearance that we should desire him". There was nothing in the physical appearance of Jesus that marked him out as special. If you had passed him in the street, you wouldn't have picked him out. That was the point. He was a human being just like any of us—as human as you are. But people despised him for it (**53:3**). We've turned the fact that Jesus identifies with us into a reason to reject him!

In the end humanity's contempt led him to the cross. We passed our verdict on Jesus, and that verdict was rejection. We strung him up on the cross, and the sight is so appalling that people "hide their faces" (**53:3**). We turned away from him—literally, as those who were there averted their eyes, and metaphorically, as people rejected his message. We do it still. Humanity continues to feel contempt towards Jesus. People may not reject Jesus the teacher or Jesus the moral example. But Jesus the Saviour, who comes to rescue us, and Jesus the Lord, who comes to rule us, is another matter. That Jesus—the real Jesus—people still despise and reject.

If you're a Christian, you may have felt that rejection when you have spoken of him with your friends. It certainly was Isaiah's experience. At his call he was told to proclaim:

"Be ever hearing, but never understanding;
　　be ever seeing, but never perceiving." (6:10)

In other words, Isaiah's hearers would hear his message over and over again but never "get" it. Their eyes would be blind and their ears would be deaf to the grace of God. The result is contempt for God's Servant. Isaiah had felt it. You may feel it if you speak of Christ. But what we feel is a faint shadow of the contempt Christ himself felt as he hung on the cross.

"He was despised and rejected by mankind,
　　a man of suffering, and familiar with pain." (**53:3**)

Substitution

In one sense, we have good reason to despise Jesus. What is it that we see when we look at him? Nothing special. There's "nothing in his appearance that we should desire him" (**53:2**). He doesn't look magnificent or majestic in any way. Quite the opposite. He looks appalling (**52:14**). He embodies everything we find contemptible. In Roman eyes his crucifixion marked him out as the very worst sort of criminal. In Jewish eyes he was cursed by God (Deuteronomy 21:22-23). The Greeks saw only folly; the Jews saw utter weakness (1 Corinthians 1:18-25). Can you think of anything less likely to be the Son of God or the Saviour of the world than a man hanging on a cross? How can a condemned man take away sin? How can a dying man bring life? How can a defeated man restore God's reign?

But here is the magnificent twist:

"Surely he took up our pain
    and bore our suffering,
yet we considered him punished by God,
    stricken by him, and afflicted.
But he was pierced for our transgressions,
    he was crushed for our iniquities;
the punishment that brought us peace was on him,
    and by his wounds we are healed." (Isaiah **53:4-5**)

To us it looks like Jesus is being punished by God. But right at the heart of this song is this amazing truth: while it is true that Jesus is being punished by God, it is not for his sins but for ours. It looks to us as if Jesus is "stricken" by God—as if God is writing him off. But it's *our* sin for which he dies and it's *our* salvation that he secures.

The central idea here is substitution. It's an idea right at the heart of our salvation. Jesus is our substitute. He died in our place. Consider the language Isaiah uses:

"*He* took up *our* pain
    and bore *our* suffering …

he was pierced for *our* transgressions,

he was crushed for *our* iniquities." (**53:4-5**)

Each time the crime is ours (our pain, our suffering, our transgressions, our iniquities), and each time the suffering is his (he took, he bore, he was pierced, he was crushed). "These words, OUR, US, FOR US," wrote the great **Reformer** Martin Luther, "should be written in gold letters. Whoever does not believe this is not a Christian" ("Lectures on Isaiah 53", *The Annotated Luther Volume 6: The Interpretation of Scripture,* p 358).

It's not just that Jesus shared the natural consequences of the human condition. This is a **judicial** act. The word "transgression" means breaking a law: in this case, God's law. "The punishment that brought us peace was on him", says **53:5**. God passed sentence on our sin, and that sentence was borne by Christ. The theological term for this is "penal substitution" ("penal" as in "penalty"). It means paying the penalty of sin in the place of another. Jesus endured the judicial wrath of God in our place.

God's **attributes** cannot be played off one against another. He doesn't stop being holy so he can show mercy. He doesn't suspend his justice to extend forgiveness to his people. But through the substitutionary death of his Son, God is true to every aspect of his character—showing mercy while remaining just (Romans 3:25-26). Here are **theologians** John Stott and C.E.B. Cranfield on the substitutionary nature of the cross:

"God must 'satisfy himself', responding to the realities of human rebellion in a way that is perfectly consonant with his character. This internal necessity is our fixed starting-point. In consequence, it would be impossible for us sinners to remain eternally the sole objects of his holy love, since he cannot both punish and pardon us at the same time. Hence the second necessity, namely substitution. The only way for God's holy love to be satisfied is for his holiness to be directed in judgment upon his appointed substitute, in order that his love may be directed towards us in forgiveness. The substitute bears the penalty, that we sinners may receive the pardon."

(John Stott, *The Cross of Christ*, p 158)

"God, because in his mercy he willed to forgive sinful men, and, being truly merciful, willed to forgive them righteously, that is, without in any way condoning their sin, purposed to direct against his very self in the person of his Son the full weight of that righteous wrath which they deserved."

(C. E. B. Cranfield, *The Epistle to the Romans, Volume One*, p 217)

Our pain, suffering, transgressions, iniquities and punishment are all transferred to Jesus. And in exchange we receive peace and healing (Isaiah **53:5**). Jesus gets what we deserve, while we get what he deserves. It's as if we've been struggling under a heavy load and Jesus has come, lifted the burden from us and carried it himself. Except that this load is one that ultimately crushes whoever bears it. Isaiah **53:4-6** forms the central section of Isaiah's poem. But the act it describes is also the centrepiece of the Bible story, of our salvation, of the course of human history, of the hope of God's people. Everything turns on an amazing act of substitution.

> This is the centrepiece of the Bible story, of our salvation, of the course of human history.

How did Isaiah see this? What led him to express these ideas so clearly? Perhaps Isaiah saw the cross through a direct, Spirit-given vision. Or perhaps he recognised the logic of substitution throughout the Bible story. Perhaps it was a bit of both. In these words the Spirit revealed how our salvation would be achieved. But it didn't come out of the blue. It was not without precedent. Isaiah had pictures and parallels to connect it to. Substitution was there at the beginning when God made clothes for Adam and Eve out of animal skin; something had to die for the shame of human sin to be covered (Genesis 3:21). The idea of substitution was there when

Abraham was about to kill Isaac,but an angel told him to stop and kill a ram "instead of his son" (Genesis 22:13). Substitution was there in the first Passover when the Lord killed every firstborn child throughout Egypt but passed over Hebrew homes with blood daubed on their lintels (Exodus 11 – 13). The the Passover lamb died in the place of the firstborn so they could go free. Substitution was there in the sacrifices of Israel (Leviticus 1 – 15). Day after day the price of sin was paid in blood, but not the Israelites' blood. An animal died in their place. When Isaiah says the servant "*bore* the sin of many" in **53:12**, it's the word used to describe the scapegoat on the Day of Atonement. This was the annual festival in the Israelite calendar when atonement was made for the sin of the people. Two goats were chosen. One of them was sacrificed, dying as a substitute in the place of the people. The other was driven out into the desert, signifying that, as a result of this sacrifice, the sin of the people was being carried away over the horizon (Leviticus 16:22).

As a result of this great act of substitution, the cross has "brought us peace" (Isaiah **53:5**). Isaiah is not talking about an inner calm—though that may be one of the fruits of the peace of which he speaks. Isaiah is talking about reconciliation with God. Sin is an act of rebellion. We have become God's enemies. But Christ has made peace between humanity and God.

All of this means our verdict on Christ rebounds on us. **53:3** says Jesus was "rejected by mankind". All of us at one time joined in this rejection. We formed our view of Jesus and decided that we didn't like what we saw. But this view of Jesus was not accurate. The version of Jesus that we were rejecting was not the real Jesus. That's the message of the fourth stanza (**53:7-9**). Again and again it proclaims Christ's innocence. Twice in **53:7** it says, "He did not open his mouth" (see John 19:8-10). Christ could have defended his innocence, but he refused to do so. Instead, he willingly gave himself up to this fate for our sakes. "Who of his generation protested?" asks Isaiah **53:8**. Jesus' various trials added up to a blatant act of injustice, but no one raised any objections. Think of the **Passion** narratives.

The religious leaders can't find two witnesses whose stories agree. His disciples don't stand by him. Peter keeps quiet, except to disown Jesus. The crowd chooses to release Barabbas instead of Jesus, even though the guilt of Barabbas is clear. Pilate says he can find no crime of which Jesus is guilty, and yet condemns him anyway. And so Jesus died, "though he had done no violence, nor was any deceit in his mouth" (**53:9**; see 1 Peter 2:21-24).

We see Jesus hanging on the cross, conclude that he was guilty of a great crime and therefore reject him. "We considered him punished by God," says Isaiah **53:4**. "But he was pierced for our transgressions" (**53:5**). So when we reject Jesus, we are not actually rejecting his true character. Instead, what we are rejecting is the fact of our sin—our sin as it is borne by Jesus. The verdict we pass on Jesus is a verdict that rebounds on us. The weakness and shame that we see in him is *our* weakness and shame. The punishment inflicted on him by God for which we so despise him is the punishment *we* deserve.

But when the Spirit of God opens our eyes, what we see at the cross is pure love. Jesus offered himself, freely, willingly, for us, taking up our pain, bearing our suffering, crushed on our behalf, so that by his wounds we might be healed.

Questions for reflection

1. What's your experience of people's reactions to Jesus? How does Isaiah 52:13 – 53:12 help you understand those reactions?

2. What do you personally find most moving about this passage?

3. Reflect on your own behaviour and life in the light of this passage. Do you take sin seriously enough? Do you know the forgiveness and healing that can be found in Christ?

PART TWO

Glory

At the cross humanity passed its verdict on Jesus, and its verdict was condemnation. But the cross is not the end of the story. Isaiah **53:10** says:

> "Yet it was the LORD's will to crush him and cause him to suffer,
>> and though the LORD makes his life an offering for sin,
> he will see his offspring and prolong his days,
>> and the will of the LORD will prosper in his hand."

At the resurrection the LORD gives his verdict on Christ—and his verdict is vindication. It's not just Christ's innocence that is vindicated. His guilt, as it were, is vindicated. What I mean is this. Jesus died under the judgment of God. He died the death of a guilty person. He took our guilt upon himself and made it his own. He removed it from us and bore it himself. And now, through the resurrection, that act has been vindicated. God confirms that Christ has borne our guilt in our place. "God made him who had no sin to be sin for us, so that in him we might become the righteousness of God" (2 Corinthians 5:21). It turns out it was the LORD's will that he should suffer in our place. The death of Christ was the centrepiece of a divine plan stretching beyond time into eternity. The Son covenanted to offer himself as a sacrifice for our sins, and the Father covenanted to accept that sacrifice. The glorious sign that the Father has accepted the sacrifice is the resurrection of Jesus. "After he has suffered," says Isaiah **53:11**, "he will see the light of life and be satisfied".

The song circles back to where it started in **52:13**: "See, my servant will act wisely; he will be raised and lifted up and highly exalted". We've met this language before in Isaiah. At his call, we're told in 6:1, Isaiah "saw the Lord, high and exalted, seated on a throne". Jesus, the Son of God, who became human, who was despised and rejected, who was disfigured beyond recognition, who descended to the grave, is now lifted and exalted alongside God. The world falls silent as Jesus is vindicated (**52:15**). What looks like utter folly is actually true wisdom. "My servant will act wisely", says **52:13**. The cross appears to all the world like a failed plan or pointless gesture. But in fact it is the power and wisdom of God (1 Corinthians 1:18-25).

But here's a second twist. The apostle John quotes from this song in John 12:38, and a few verses earlier he echoes the language of Isaiah **52:13**. Jesus says, "And I, when I am lifted up from the earth, will draw all people to myself". Then John himself adds by way of explanation, "He said this to show the kind of death he was going to die" (John 12:32-33; see also John 3:14-15). Jesus is lifted up, but John is not referring to his resurrection, nor to his ascension. Jesus is lifted on the cross. This is his glory in John's Gospel. It's a strange kind of pun. Crucifixion literally involved lifting someone up so everyone could see them dying. Presumably it was intended as a deterrent. So Jesus was literally lifted up on the cross. But this lifting up represents his exaltation. This is Christ's glory because through his death Christ will save many people. That is why Jesus says, "I, when I am lifted up from the earth, will draw all people to myself" (John 12:32). In the end, *we* are his glory. We are the display of the depths of his love and the power of salvation.

This is what we see in the song of Isaiah 53. The song begins with a double reference to "many":

"Just as there were *many* who were appalled at him …
so he will sprinkle *many* nations." (**52:14-15**)

Sprinkling here is an act of purification (Numbers 8:6-7; Leviticus 8:10-11; 14:15-16). Many people rejected Jesus, but through that rejection many people will be saved. This double "many" is then echoed at the end of the song:

"By his knowledge my righteous servant will justify *many* …
For he bore the sin of *many*." (Isaiah **53:11-12**)

Many people will be made right with God through the work of Jesus. We see the evidence of this all across the pages of history and all around the world. The vindication of Jesus is taking shape in local churches across the globe—local churches like yours. Every time someone is saved, the triumph of the death and resurrection of Jesus is confirmed once more.

Isaiah **52:15b** says:

"For what they were not told, they will see,
    and what they have not heard, they will understand."

If you're reading Isaiah carefully, this is an amazing moment. As we saw when we looked at Isaiah 6, Isaiah's message was to be:

"Be ever hearing, but never understanding;
    be ever seeing, but never perceiving." (6:9)

But now that message kicks into reverse. A day is coming when people who were not told will see and people who have not heard will understand—people like me and you. Through the preaching of his word, God has come and found you. And through your preaching of his word, God comes to yet more people and finds them. This is why it should be our ambition to see Christ preached where he is not known, as Paul reminds us in Romans 15:20-21, where he quotes Isaiah **52:15**.

Chapters 54 – 55 extend this idea. Isaiah calls on a barren woman to sing because she is about to bear many children (54:1). It's a picture of God's barren people about to see many converts. So in Isaiah 55:1 the invitation goes out:

"Come, all you who are thirsty,
    come to the waters;
and you who have no money,
    come, buy and eat!
Come, buy wine and milk
    without money and without cost."

The key point is that this is the invitation that flows from the work of the cross. This is the fruit of the suffering of the Servant in **52:13 – 53:12**. And this is the invitation that comes to us in the gospel.

Isaiah **53:12** says, "Therefore I will give him a portion among the great, and he will divide the spoils with the strong". The word "great" is a bit misleading. While the word can mean "great", it can also mean "many" or "numerous" (Exodus 1:7). That is what it has meant so far in this song. So this is not about the servant cosying up to the great and the good. The "many" are "his offspring" and those whom he has "justified" (Isaiah **53:10-11**). It also helps to realise that the words "give", "portion" and "divide" are all the same word in Hebrew. Put this all together and we get this more literal translation of **53:12**:

"Therefore I will allocate many as an allocation to him
and he will allocate the strong as plunder."

God does the allocating in the first line; God gives many people to Jesus. The Servant does the allocating in the second line. Just like a triumphant king distributing the fruit of his success among his loyal retainers, Jesus distributes the rewards of his success among his people. Jesus invites us to share his victory.

What's the Servant's reward? Us. God's people. You and me. Why? "Because he poured out his life … he bore the sin of many" (**53:12**). His death worked! It secures our salvation, and it secures his victory.

What's our reward? At the moment we're besieged and beset by the world around us. In the West we're mocked and marginalised. Elsewhere in the world Christians are persecuted and imprisoned. But the strong don't win. *We win!* In fact, we've already won because Jesus has risen from the dead. The enemies of God did their worst, and it was not enough to overcome Jesus. They can do their worst to us, but nothing will separate us from the love of Christ (Romans 8:35-39).

Those who feel crushed

When Isaiah stood before the holiness of God, he felt utterly ruined (6:5). He felt as if he was being crushed by the holiness of God. But he was *not* crushed. An angel brought a coal from the altar to cleanse his sin. Now listen to what God says in Isaiah 57:15:

"For this is what the high and exalted One says—
he who lives for ever, whose name is holy …"

Who is this? Who is the "high and exalted One ... whose name is holy"? It's the Lord whom Isaiah saw in the temple. Isaiah 6:1 describes him as "high and exalted"—exactly the same words—and the seraphim name him as "holy". So here is the God that Isaiah saw, who brought Isaiah to the brink of ruin, the three-times holy God before whom even angels cover their faces. And what does he say?

> "I live in a high and holy place,
>> but also with the one who is contrite and lowly in spirit,
>> to revive the spirit of the lowly
>> and to revive the heart of the contrite." (57:15)

It's literally "I live with the crushed". The same word is used elsewhere to speak of people returning to the dust (Psalm 90:3). The high God revives those who are crushed.

How can the high One and the holy One dwell among sinful, broken people like us? To see the answer, we need to recognize that the same word is used in the song of Isaiah 53. Isaiah says of Jesus, "He was *crushed* for our iniquities" (**53:5**). He says, "It was the LORD's will to *crush* him and cause him to suffer" (**53:10**). Standing in God's presence, Isaiah felt as if he was being crushed. But he was not crushed. Instead, the person who was crushed was Jesus. At the cross Jesus placed himself between us and the holiness of God. As a result, Jesus was ruined in our place. The very fabric of his being unravelled.

> Isaiah felt crushed. But he was not crushed. The person who was crushed was Jesus.

So now, through Jesus, the exalted One dwells among those who have been brought low. The holy One comes to revive the flagging hearts of contrite sinners. Do you want to ascend up into the presence of God? Then lower yourself. Leave your excuses, your pride, your claims at the door, and humble yourself before him.

Or perhaps you already feel crushed. Your guilt presses down on you. Or your fears overwhelm you. Or your confidence has evaporated. Do not despair. You are in a good place, for it is the place where God dwells. There is no need to hide your sin or pretend that you've got it all together. For God sees his Son, "crushed for our iniquities", and he says to us, "I live ... with the one who is contrite and lowly in spirit". He comes to us through his word and through his **sacraments** "to revive the spirit of the lowly and to revive the heart of the contrite".

Standing before the cross is like standing in a hall of mirrors where you're made to look fatter or thinner, or turned upside down. The difference is that the cross reflects back an image of our true selves. It turns the way we perceive ourselves upside down. If we think we're high and mighty, the cross exposes our desperate need. But if we feel crushed and lowly, the cross lifts us up into the very presence of God.

Questions for reflection

1. Is it your ambition to see Christ preached where he is not yet known? What steps could you take to contribute to missionary and evangelistic work?

2. In what sense do we share in Jesus' victory? When life doesn't feel very victorious, what hope is there?

3. How does reflecting on the cross challenge and help you personally?

12. THE LIGHT OF GOD'S SERVANTS

FOCUS: ISAIAH 60

A few miles from my home is the self-proclaimed "best view in England". You look from the beginning of the Yorkshire Moors National Park across the Vale of York to the beginnings of the Yorkshire Dales on the horizon. At night the vale is filled with little pockets of light representing all the villages in between the Moors and Dales (including my town). When you look with spiritual eyes, whether you stand there in the day or the night, you see deep spiritual darkness. And you might despair. Perhaps you have some equivalent view—a point where you can look across your town or city. Isaiah 60 is an encouragement to hope.

In chapters 40 – 55 Isaiah looked ahead to the time when Babylon would enslave God's people. Isaiah promised freedom, but his vision of salvation looked beyond liberation from Babylon to liberation from sin and death through Jesus. In chapters 56 – 66 Isaiah looks ahead to the return of the Jews to Judea to reconstruct their country, which took place under Ezra and Nehemiah. But again Isaiah also looks beyond the return from exile.

Although there are different ways of configuring it, Isaiah 56 – 66 appears to be chiastic, with the first and last sections paralleling one another, then the second and penultimate sections, and so on:

A. Salvation will come to the nations (56:1-8)

  B. Comfort for the contrite amid false worshippers (56:9 – 58:14)

    C. A prayer for forgiveness (59:1-15)

      D. God himself comes to establish justice (59:15-21)

        E. Zion is restored as a witness to the nations (60)

        F. The Spirit anoints the Servant to proclaim good news (61)

        E'. Zion is restored as a witness to the nations (62)

      D'. God himself comes to establish justice (63:1-7)

    C'. A prayer for forgiveness (63:7 – 64:12)

  B'. Comfort for the contrite amid false worshippers (65:1 – 66:16)

A'. Salvation will come to the nations (66:17-24)

At the heart of this chiastic structure is the anointing ("messiah"-ing) of the prophet or the Servant or God's people to proclaim good news:

"The Spirit of the Sovereign LORD is on me,

  because the LORD has anointed me

  to proclaim good news to the poor." (61:1; 59:21)

It's a passage that Jesus applies to himself in Luke 4:16-21. The key word is "proclaim". Isaiah 40 – 55 described how the Servant redeems God's people. Now chapters 56 – 66 describe how God's people are gathered through the proclamation of the Servant's redemption.

So these chapters are a promise of a worldwide church created through a worldwide mission—through the proclamation of the good news of the new exodus won through the Servant's **vicarious** death. They come to a climax, as we shall see, in the inclusion of people from all nations in the new creation.

Reader's guide

Isaiah 56 - 57

One of the themes of this section is the call for God's people to be a community of justice. The section begins, "Maintain justice and do what is right" (56:1-2). In this new community, **eunuchs** will be fruitful, and foreigners will be included (56:3-8). But this is not how it was in Isaiah's day (56:9 – 57:13), nor is it how the world around us is today. No one cares when good people are silenced while evil people prosper (57:1-2). People mock God's ways (57:3-4) and sacrifice their children in pursuit of their lust (57:5). They prefer **occult** practices (57:6-8) and worldly alliances (57:9-10) to trust in God. Descending to "the very realm of the dead" (57:9) is probably a reference to making an alliance with Egypt, which Isaiah has already mocked as "a covenant with death" (28:15). The coming of God's judgment is ignored as people say, "Tomorrow will be like today, or even far better" (56:12). God offers his presence and his peace to those who are lowly and contrite, but his offer is ignored (57:14-21).

Isaiah 58

The people complain that God is ignoring their religious performances (58:1-3). But in God's sight, religious performance that is not connected to obedient lives is meaningless (58:3-7). "Is not this the kind of fasting I have chosen," says God in 58:6: "to loose the chains of injustice and untie the cords of the yoke?" When God's people do justice, then they will be a light to the nations (58:8-10). They will be blessed by God, and they will be a blessing to others (58:11-14). "If you spend yourselves on behalf of the hungry and satisfy the needs of the oppressed, then your light will rise in the darkness" (58:10).

Isaiah 59

In Isaiah 59 God looks across the land and sees injustice. "Their deeds are evil deeds, and acts of violence are in their hands" (59:6). "So justice is far from us" and "truth is nowhere to be found" (59:9, 15). What makes this worse is that "no one calls for justice" (59:4). "The LORD looked and was displeased ..." says Isaiah, "that there was no one to intervene" (59:15-16). So the LORD himself intervenes. Isaiah pictures God as a warrior, putting on armour to fight for justice (59:15-20). God, in the person of Jesus, himself comes to fight and bring light.

Isaiah 60

In chapter 60 the imagery of light comes to the fore. God will light up his people so they can be a light to the world (60:1-9). This is fulfilled in Jesus and the church, who are both described in the New Testament as "the light of the world" (John 8:12; Matthew 5:14). Isaiah paints a picture of a glorious future which is ultimately fulfilled in the new Jerusalem (60:10-22; Revelation 21).

Jesus is the light of the world

Isaiah 60 begins:

"Arise, shine, for your light has come,
    and the glory of the LORD rises upon you.
See, darkness covers the earth
    and thick darkness is over the peoples,
but the LORD rises upon you
    and his glory appears over you." (**60:1-2**)

"Your light has come." And what is that light? The LORD himself. "The LORD rises upon you and his glory appears over you."

Back in 9:2 Isaiah had said, "The people walking in darkness have seen a great light; on those living in the land of deep darkness a light has dawned". Light is coming because "a child is born … a son is given" (9:6). God is coming in the person of his Son to bring light.

Then it's as if there was a huge pause in history until, in John 8:12, Jesus said, "I am the light of the world. Whoever follows me will never walk in darkness, but will have the light of life." Isaiah has his fingerprints all over the New Testament, and this statement is no exception. "Walking in darkness" is the language of Isaiah 9:2 and 59:9. "The light of the world" is from Isaiah 42:6 and 49:6—that's how the promised Servant is described. "The light of life" is taken from 53:11. All the pain of living in darkness expressed by Isaiah and all the anticipation of the promise of light is compressed into one wonderful declaration from Jesus.

Darkness covers the earth. Humanity is groping in the dark, looking for answers. We live furtive lives under the cloak of darkness. And in that darkness evil breeds, creating a nighttime of fear. But Jesus comes into the world, and light bursts into our darkness. "Your light has come." The glory of the LORD appears, and his glory is seen in Jesus. Or think of your own darkness—the grief or conflict or disappointment or bitterness that shadows your soul. "Your light has come," and his name is Jesus.

The church is the light of the world

What is the impact on God's people? "Then you will look and be radiant" (**60:5**). Not only is Jesus the light of the world, but the *community* of Jesus is the light of the world. Light shines on us, and as a result we light up! We radiate, reflecting the glory of Jesus. God describes us as "the work of my hands, for the display of my splendour" (**60:21**).

When I was a boy, I had a luminous watch. The numbers and hands were painted with a special paint that absorbed light energy and then radiated it back. I would shine my torch under the bed covers at night and marvel at the lit-up face when I switched the torch off. All this, of course, was before people thought of putting batteries in watches! In a similar kind of way we are luminous people. The glory of Jesus shines on us, and we radiate that glory to a dark world. Isaiah continues in **60:5**: "Your heart will throb and swell with joy". We talk about someone's face "lighting up" when they have received great news. We hear the good news of Jesus, and our lives light up with joy. We become enthusiasts, and enthusiasts radiate their enthusiasm.

Chapters 40 – 55 are full of references to the Servant of the LORD. "Here is my servant," says God in 42:1. All the time there is one Servant (singular). But after Isaiah has described the Servant's work of salvation through suffering, that changes. For example:

■ "This is the heritage of the *servants* of the LORD, and this is their vindication from me," declares the LORD. (54:17)

■ "I will bring forth descendants from Jacob, and from Judah those who will possess my mountains; my chosen people will inherit them, and there will *my servants* live." (65:9)

■ "*My servants* will sing out of the joy of their hearts." (65:14)

Through the work of Jesus, we *all* become God's servants (plural).

Isaiah has in mind not just the people of Israel. In 56:6-7 he says:

"And foreigners who bind themselves to the LORD
    to minister to him,
to love the name of the LORD,
    and to be his *servants* ...
these I will bring to my holy mountain
    and give them joy in my house of prayer."

It's not just that Israel will be a light to the nations, but people *from* the nations will be a light *to* the nations. Isaiah **60:4** invites us to...

"Lift up your eyes and look about you:
    all assemble and come to you;
your sons come from afar,
    and your daughters are carried on the hip."

We can be **parochial** in outlook with our heads down, focused only on what is going on around us. But just as he did in 43:6, Isaiah wants us to lift up our eyes and see people flooding into the church around the world.

In chapter 60 Isaiah is describing the fulfilment of his vision in 2:2-4. There he looked forward to a day when Jerusalem would be a city on a hill and "all nations will stream to it". God will settle disputes; swords will be turned into ploughshares and spears into pruning hooks. "Let us walk in the light of the LORD," he says by way of application (2:5). This is exactly what is happening in chapter **60:3**: "Nations will come to your light, and kings to the brightness of your dawn". Isaiah begins to list some of the nations who come in **60:8-9**:

"Who are these that fly along like clouds,
    like doves to their nests?

Surely the islands look to me;
in the lead are the ships of Tarshish,
bringing your children from afar,
with their silver and gold,
to the honour of the LORD your God,
the Holy One of Israel,
for he has endowed you with splendour."

Through the mission of the church, people from every nation are being drawn to Christ. They are becoming sons and daughters of God (**60:4** and 43:6). They are becoming part of God's people. But don't take my word for it. Listen to the words of Jesus in Matthew 5:14: "You are the light of the world. A town built on a hill cannot be hidden." This is Jesus, the one who says, "I am the light of the world" (John 8:12). But now he says, "*You* are the light of the world." And he's not talking to the brightest and best but to his motley crew of disciples. He's talking to people like you and me. We are the light of the world. We are a city built on a hill—a reference to Isaiah 2:2-5. We are the fulfilment of Isaiah's vision. The nations come to Jerusalem to discover God's ways. But they don't come to *geographic* Jerusalem; they come to *spiritual* Jerusalem—to the church scattered across the globe.

> Walk in the light; shine with the light of God. Bring glory to your Father.

What's the application? The application in 2:5 is, "Come, descendants of Jacob, let us walk in the light of the LORD". The application in **60:1** is "Arise, shine, for your light has come". And the application in Matthew 5:16 is essentially the same: "Let your light shine before others, that they may see your good deeds and glorify your Father in heaven". The same vision is being picked up and developed. Walk in the light; shine with the light of God. Do good deeds that bring glory to your Father.

Jesus says in Matthew 5:15, "Neither do people light a lamp and put it under a bowl. Instead they put it on its stand, and it gives light to everyone in the house." I recently bought a new desk lamp. I love it. Even with my failing eyes, I can now clearly see all my work spread across my desk. But imagine I bought that light, plugged it in, switched it on and then put a box over it. That would be crazy. The glory of the LORD has risen upon you in the person of Jesus. God's light has lit up your life. So don't hide your light under a bowl. Don't shut it up in a church building. Put it on a stand. Get out into your street, your neighbourhood and your town. Walk in the light, radiate God's glory and proclaim Christ.

Questions for reflection

1. In what ways do you feel you are living in darkness? How does Isaiah 60 give you hope?

2. Do you tend to focus only on what is going on immediately around you? What can you do to lift your eyes to God's work around the world?

3. What will it look like for you to radiate God's glory in the coming weeks?

PART TWO

Isaiah calls us to walk in the light of the Lord so that the ways of the Lord are made known to the nations. We do this not only through the words we say but the lives we live. One of the big themes in Isaiah 56 – 60 is the importance of justice. From chapter 1 onwards Isaiah has condemned injustice (1:15-17). But now he puts forward a positive vision of a community of justice displaying God's glory. The section begins, "Maintain justice and do what is right" (56:1).

Again, this call for social justice is linked to a promise that God's people will be a light to the nations (58:8-10). This kind of community will be richly blessed by God (58:11-14) and be a rich blessing to others. "If you spend yourselves on behalf of the hungry and satisfy the needs of the oppressed, then your light will rise in the darkness" (58:10). It's not just our words that witness to Christ but also our life as the Christian community. Our churches are to be communities of justice and care. As we welcome refugees, care for the marginalised, provide debt counselling, look after the elderly, set up social enterprises, visit the sick and adopt children, light shines in the darkness.

Light of the new world

Have you ever said anything like, "It was only the thought of ... that kept me going"? "It was only the thought of a cup of tea that kept me going on my walk in the rain." "It was only the thought of seeing you again that kept me going while I was away." Isaiah 60 is a vision to help us keep going.

"The sun will no more be your light by day,
    nor will the brightness of the moon shine on you,
  for the LORD will be your everlasting light,
    and your God will be your glory.
  Your sun will never set again,
    and your moon will wane no more;

the LORD will be your everlasting light,
and your days of sorrow will end." (**60:19-20**)

Isaiah has said our light will come. We've seen how this happens in the person of Christ. As a result, the church becomes a light to the world, and the nations join God's people. It's all so exciting. But Isaiah keeps on going. There's no stopping him. There'll be so much light, he says, we won't even need the sun!

But Isaiah is not getting carried away with his **rhetoric**. He is moving beyond this world and into the next world. Or, perhaps more accurately, he just sees the future. It's us who can now recognise that the new age began with the resurrection of Jesus but is not yet fulfilled. We can see that Isaiah's vision of the future in fact happens in two stages: with the first and second comings of Jesus. So it's not always clear which elements of Isaiah's vision belong to which phase—not least because we're talking about two ages that overlap. The old age of darkness still continues, but the new age of light has already dawned. What we as followers of Christ experience in history is not some interim arrangement. It really is a foretaste of the coming age.

Culture matters

Isaiah's vision here in chapter 60 shapes John's vision of the new Jerusalem in Revelation 21:23-26:

> "The city does not need the sun or the moon to shine on it, for the glory of God gives it light, and the Lamb is its lamp. The nations will walk by its light, and the kings of the earth will bring their splendour into it. On no day will its gates ever be shut, for there will be no night there. The glory and honour of the nations will be brought into it."

John says, "The city does not need the sun or the moon to shine on it, for the glory of God gives it light, and the Lamb is its lamp" (Revelation 21:23). That's what Isaiah said in **60:19-20** (as we've seen). John says, "The nations will walk by its light" (Revelation 21:24). That's the language of Isaiah 2:5. One day Jesus will light up all of creation with his glory. But the parallels don't end there. John says, "On no day will its gates ever be shut, for there will be no night there" (Revelation 21:25). This idea is taken from **60:11-12**, where Isaiah said, "Your gates will always stand open, they will never be shut, day or night".

Isaiah **60:11** continues, "so that". There's a reason the gates are always open. It is "so that people may bring you the wealth of the nations". And again John picks this up. He says, "The kings of the earth will bring their splendour into it" (Revelation 21:25). Isaiah 60 is an inventory of the world's wealth being brought to God's people.

"The wealth on the seas will be brought to you,
    to you the riches of the nations will come ...
And all from Sheba will come,
    bearing gold and incense ...
All Kedar's flocks will be gathered to you,
    the rams of Nebaioth will serve you ...
Surely the islands look to me;
    in the lead are the ships of Tarshish ...
    with their silver and gold,
to the honour of the LORD your God ...
Foreigners will rebuild your walls,
    and their kings will serve you ...
so that people may bring you the wealth of the nations ...
The glory of Lebanon will come to you."

                              (**60:5**, **6**, **7**, **9**, **10**, **11**, **13**)

We have met this idea before in Isaiah. In Isaiah 23 the prophet announces the fall of Tyre—the greatest trading nation of its day. But Isaiah also speaks of her restoration; once again she will "ply her trade with all the kingdoms on the face of the earth" (23:17). This time "her profit and her earnings will be set apart for the LORD" (23:18). Under **Solomon's** reign the kings of the earth brought their splendour to Jerusalem (1 Kings 4:20-21). But when Israel turned from God, the nations no longer brought their splendour to

Jerusalem. Instead they came to plunder Jerusalem, robbing the city of its splendour (1 Kings 11:23-25; 14:24-28). Isaiah 23:18 looks forward to the rebuilding of the temple, when Tyre would again provide materials (Ezra 3:7). But Isaiah looks beyond this, too, to the day when the trading wealth of the nations will be used not for selfish, proud human ends, but for the glory of God and the enrichment of his people (Isaiah **60:5**, 15-18). In the book of Revelation John picks up this idea. But in John's vision there is no temple in the new Jerusalem because the whole world is a temple-city in which God dwells with his people. And all that is good in the economies and cultures of the nations will find a place in the new Jerusalem (Revelation 21:24-26).

> Human cultures are not trashed at the end of history; they are fulfilled.

This vision of the climax of history gives great value to what we do in history. The temple-city is so full of divine glory that there's no need for the sun or moon (21:23). And yet amazingly there is space for *human* glory: "The glory and honour of the nations will be brought into it" (21:26). The temple-city doesn't *replace* the glories of this world; instead it *fulfils* them. The best of human culture is incorporated into the city. Quite how this works is unclear. But there seems to be some measure of cultural continuity between this age and the next. Artistic endeavour and social action can be of eternal consequence. What is clear is the value this gives to human cultural activity. Human cultures are not trashed at the end of history; they are fulfilled.

This means culture matters. It is true that the gospel is gloriously transcultural. It brings people of different races and cultures together, so that what unites us (Christ) is more important than what divides us (cultural differences). We are all one in Christ Jesus. Christian mission must witness to the reconciling nature of the gospel and this wonderful vision of people from every nation, tribe and tongue gathered around the throne of the Lamb. But we must be careful how we do this. The gospel is still to be expressed in local cultures. The danger is that those who are from a dominant culture can use talk of the way the gospel transcends culture to impose—often unwittingly—their cultural norms on others. This means that sometimes we have to go out of our way to ensure minority cultures are included, respected and expressed. In practice this means ensuring that within your church life you have ways of expressing *both* (1) our unity in the gospel across cultures and (2) the value of cultural diversity and local cultural expression. How you do this will be context specific and vary over time. The key is to ensure that both unity and diversity are expressed in the life of your church and especially in its leadership.

When your light is dim

Isaiah is describing the mission of the church. But he's also describing the final glory of the church. You and I are called to be a light to the nations—in our homes, our workplaces and our neighbourhoods. Isaiah 60 and Revelation 21 describe the culmination of that witness. This is where it leads. Your light may seem dim. There may be days when it flickers on and off. The darkness may sometimes feel overwhelming. But this is the outcome. One day our witness—your witness—will result in a city of light with people from every nation. Listen to the encouragement of Isaiah **60:22**:

"The least of you will become a thousand,
the smallest a mighty nation.
I am the LORD;
in its time I will do this swiftly."

It can be tempting to feel ashamed at how small we are. When people ask about our church or ministry, we tend to cite numbers at the top end. We want people to think we're successful. But many of us serve in situations where numbers are small and progress is slow. Isaiah is not promising imminent growth. But he is saying that our contribution matters and the triumph of the gospel is certain. One day we will be part of a congregation beyond number. When I look at the vale in which I live, I see darkness. I say, paraphrasing Isaiah **60:2**, "Darkness covers the vale and thick darkness is over the peoples." But I can also say, "Arise, shine, for your light has come, and the glory of the LORD rises upon you" (**60:1**).

Questions for reflection

1. What can you do to be light in the darkness as a local church?

2. What is your attitude towards other cultures? Think about the church ministries or evangelistic work you are involved in. How can you celebrate cultural diversity while making the gospel paramount?

3. What will you pray for your church, your nation and the world as a result of reading Isaiah 60?

13. THE PRAYER OF GOD'S SERVANTS

FOCUS: ISAIAH 64

A few years ago I visited a church in a city called Gjilan in Kosovo. Each week members of the church went up on the hill overlooking the town and prayed their hearts out for their city. I also once visited a church in Ethiopia with wooden benches on an earth floor and a tarpaulin roof. When they started to pray, I felt poor. When I lived in London, our church formed a link with some Brazilian missionaries. To pray with them was very special. They stood to pray and their times of prayer were full of energy. One person was clearly praying, but everyone else was adding to their prayer with cries of praise or **petition**.

What creates a praying church or a praying person? What sustains an energy for prayer? Isaiah 64 gives a powerful motive to pray with passion. That motive is the recognition that we need God to revive our hearts, our church, our nation.

Another exodus

Isaiah 64 begins with the plea "Oh, that you would rend the heavens and come down" (**64:1**). In 63:15 Isaiah called on God to "*look* down from heaven". Now he calls on God to "*come* down" from heaven (emphasis added). Isaiah is looking ahead to the defeat of Judah by the Babylonians, the destruction of Jerusalem, the ruin of the temple and the exile of the people. In **64:10-11** he says Jerusalem is "a desolation" and the temple "has been burned with fire" (see also 63:18).

When Isaiah himself speaks, that hasn't happened yet. It would be another two centuries before Jerusalem would be destroyed. But Isaiah has predicted it, and now he imagines what it will be like for the returning exiles. Perhaps he imagines himself looking over Jerusalem—just like my friends in war-torn Gjilan—and what he sees is a wasteland (**64:10**). "All that we treasured lies in ruins" (**64:11**). So he cries out in pain, "Oh, that you would rend the heavens and come down" (**64:1**). In effect his prayer is *Come down; get stuck in; put things right*. In 63:1-6 Isaiah described God drenched in blood; there was no one to see justice done, so God himself had come down to carry out judgment. But that moment has not yet come. Isaiah prays with passion because he (fore-)sees the need.

Reader's guide

Isaiah 61

In 61:1 the Servant is anointed by God's Spirit to proclaim good news. It's a passage that Jesus applies to himself in Luke 4:16-21. As a result of the suffering and triumph of the Servant, we now proclaim good news of healing, freedom, comfort and joy (Isaiah 61:1-3). God is going to take away the shame of his people (61: 7) and clothe us in the righteousness of Christ (61:3, 10).

Isaiah 62

In chapter 62 Isaiah promises the vindication and restoration of God's people (62:1-3). The LORD will "marry" the land, removing her shame for ever (62: 4-5). It is a promise fulfilled as Jesus dies to beautify his bride (Ephesians 5:25-27). The LORD commits himself to protect his people (Isaiah 62:8-9). God will come to dwell in Jerusalem, which will therefore be known as "the City No Longer Deserted" (62:10-12). This promise is partially fulfilled in the presence of the Spirit in the church, and fully fulfilled in the new Jerusalem, which is a described as a bride and of which it is said, "Look! God's dwelling place is now among the people, and he will dwell with them" (Revelation 21:2-3).

Isaiah 63 - 64

As in 59:15-20, God is described as a warrior coming to judge the nations (63:1-6; see Revelation 19:11-21). Isaiah then recalls the story of the first exodus from Egypt (63:7-14) and makes this the basis of a prayer asking that God will again liberate his people (63:15 – 64:12).

Isaiah 65

*The people of Judah have been "obstinate", refusing to turn to God (65:2-5). The mention of "gardens" in 65:3 is a reference to self-created forms of **pagan** worship (1:29; 66:17), while eating the "flesh of pigs" in 65:4 is a reference to the laws on **unclean food** (Leviticus 11:17). So God will give Judah the judgment they deserve (Isaiah 65:6-7, 11-17). Nevertheless, in his mercy God will save a remnant of Judah (65:8-10), and he will save people (i.e. Gentiles) who were never looking for him (65:1). In 65:17 God says, "See, I will create a new heavens and a new earth". It will be a world of joy, life, safety, abundance and peace (65:18-24).*

Isaiah 66

Isaiah condemns those who think they can contain God in a religious building or manipulate him through religious practices (66:1-3) instead of humbly trembling at his word (66:2, 5). The false worshippers will be judged (66:4-6, 15-17, 24). But a new nation will be born in a day (66:7-9) when Christ returns. God will bring joy, satisfaction, peace and comfort to true worshippers (66:10-14). People from every nation will come to worship God together (66:18-23; Revelation 7:9-10).

Isaiah also prays with passion because he knows the story of God and his people. Isaiah makes this plea on the basis of what God has done in the past. "Oh, that you would ... come down", says Isaiah **64:1**. **64:3** says, "You came down [past tense], and the mountains trembled before you". It's a reference to the exodus, when God delivered the people of Israel from slavery in Egypt and met with them at Mount

Sinai, where the mountain trembled. No one had seen anything like it before, says **64:4**.

Isaiah **64:1-4** is the climax of a plea that began back in 63:11-13:

"Then his people recalled the days of old,
the days of Moses and his people—
where is he who brought them through the sea,
with the shepherd of his flock? *[= the parting of the Red Sea]*
Where is he who set
his Holy Spirit among them, *[= the pillars of cloud and fire]*
who sent his glorious arm of power
to be at Moses' right hand, *[= the ten plagues on Egypt]*
who divided the waters before them,
to gain for himself everlasting renown,
who led them through the depths?" *[= the parting of the Red Sea again]*

What Isaiah is asking for is *another exodus*. As we have seen, God has promised a new exodus repeatedly through Isaiah's ministry. Now that promise becomes the basis of Isaiah's prayers. As he looks forward to the exile in Babylon, he sees God's people in slavery again. Even when they return from Babylon, they will still feel like slaves because they will be ruled by foreign kings. "We are yours from of old," says 63:19. But it doesn't feel like that to Isaiah. "You have not ruled over them," he continues. In other words, they are slaves to other powers. So he calls for another exodus.

A bigger problem

But immediately there's a problem. Isaiah **64:5** says God helps those who "gladly do right", but "we continued to sin". "Continued" in **64:5** is the same word as "ancient times" in **64:4**. So Isaiah is linking these verses to create a contrast. From ancient times no one has seen a God who is so faithful to his people. But from ancient times God's people have been *un*faithful. Isaiah expands on this in 65:2-5. "All day long I have held out my hands to an obstinate people," says God in

65:2. But in response the people have said, "Keep away; don't come near me" (65:5).

Here's the problem. If the contest is between Israel and the nations, **64:1-4** makes perfect sense. Here is Israel in trouble. God is on Israel's side. So Israel's enemies are God's enemies. Therefore Isaiah can say, "Come down to make your name known to your enemies and cause the nations to quake before you!" (**64:2**) Imagine the battlefield. Israel is on one side; the nations are on the other side, and it's not looking good for Israel. But then God

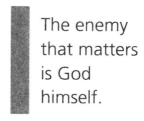

The enemy that matters is God himself.

comes down and sides with his people (**64:3**). Immediately the nations quake with fear. The nations versus Israel *plus God* looks like certain destruction for the nations. Job done!

But there's a fatal flaw in the argument—and Isaiah has already spotted it. In 63:7 Isaiah recalls "the many good things [God] has done for Israel". "Yet," says 63:10, "they rebelled and grieved his Holy Spirit. So he turned and *became their enemy* and he himself fought against them" (emphasis added). So God will "pay ... back" what they deserve (65:6-7). The battle that really matters is not Israel versus the nations but Israel versus God. Or humanity versus God. The enemy that matters is God himself.

I wonder if you've woken up to that reality yet. If I asked you what problems you were facing, I wonder what you'd say. Economic recession, government cutbacks, unemployment, marriage break-up, crime? Israel would have said the Babylonian military machine. These are all real and significant problems. But our number one problem is God. We've made God our enemy—and how can you protect yourself when God is your enemy?

Maybe you think, "No problem, I can clean up my life". Isaiah is one step ahead of you. In **64:6** he says, "All of us have become like one who is unclean, and all our righteous acts are like filthy rags". We can't clean up our lives because deep down we are unclean people. Even the good things we do are signs of our proud self-reliance. No matter how respectable we may seem, we are all enemies of God.

It's not just that we can't please God. Left to ourselves, we won't even ask him for help. Human beings are hardwired with a deep-seated bias against God.

> "No one calls on your name
>> or strives to lay hold of you;
> for you have hidden your face from us
>> and have given us over to our sins." (**64:7**)

So we're left with the question posed at the end of **64:5**: "How then can we be saved?" Let me suggest three answers to that question.

The Father's mercy

In **64:7** the situation looks hopeless. But the next word is "Yet" (**64:8**)! The story is not over; there's still more to say. "Yet you, LORD, are our Father." The God who made mountains tremble and the God who is angry at sin is our Father.

> "He said, 'Surely they are my people,
>> children who will be true to me';
> and so he became their Saviour.
> In all their distress he too was distressed,
>> and the angel of his presence saved them.
> In his love and mercy he redeemed them;
>> he lifted them up and carried them
>> all the days of old." (63:8-9)

Again, Isaiah is speaking of the exodus. It was at the beginning of the first exodus that Israel was first called "God's son" (Exodus 4:22-23). Or consider Isaiah 63:16:

> "But you are our Father,
>> though Abraham does not know us
>> or Israel acknowledge us;

you, LORD, are our Father,

our Redeemer from of old is your name."

Here are Abraham and Israel (otherwise known as Jacob)—the human fathers of the nation—and they refuse to acknowledge this dissolute bunch of people. We're to imagine Abraham saying, *They're nothing to do with me.* But not God! God is still "our Father". Isaiah reminds God: we are all your work (**64:8**), and we are all your people (**64:9**).

Isaiah **64:5** is literally "Behold, you were angry because we continued to sin". Isaiah **64:9** is literally "Behold, look now, we are all your people". "Behold" in **64:5** means that God looks and sees reasons to abandon us. "Behold" in **64:9** means that God sees a *bigger* reason to save us—his own fatherly mercy. So it is that in 65:8-10 God promises to save a remnant. And he adds, "The past troubles will be forgotten and hidden from my eyes" (65:16).

"Do not be angry beyond measure" in **64:9** has the sense of "Do not let us feel the full force of your anger". In other words, the danger is not that our punishment will *exceed* what our sin warrants, but that our punishment will *match* what our sin warrants. Our hope is that God will show mercy and find some way to avert the punishment we deserve.

The Son's rescue

As we have seen, Mark begins his Gospel in Mark 1:3 with a quote from Isaiah 40:3, where Isaiah is announcing the end of the exile. Then, a few verses later, Mark writes this:

"At that time Jesus came from Nazareth in Galilee and was baptised by John in the Jordan. Just as Jesus was coming up out of the water, he saw heaven being torn open and the Spirit descending on him like a dove. And a voice came from heaven: 'You are my Son, whom I love; with you I am well pleased.'"

(Mark 1:9-11)

Matthew and Luke both say that "heaven was opened" (Matthew 3:16; Luke 3:21). But Mark literally says that Jesus saw "the heavens being *torn* open". "Oh, that you would rend [or tear] the heavens and come down," said Isaiah **64:1**. Mark is saying that the baptism of Jesus was the moment when God responded to Isaiah's plea, as God tore the heavens open and came down to anoint his Son.

Isaiah 63 emphasises the way God set his Spirit among his people during the exodus (63:11) to guide them (63:14). In Mark, the Spirit descends on Jesus (1:10) and then sends him to be tested for 40 days in the wilderness, like Israel after the exodus (1:12-13). Not only that, but Isaiah laments the uncleanness of God's people in **64:6**, while shortly after his baptism Jesus is tackling an unclean spirit in Mark 1:21-28.

The rent heaven and the descending Spirit are signs that God himself has come in person—the person of his Son—to deliver his people.

This is because, as we have seen, *another* exodus is not enough. It wouldn't deal with the God-problem—the fact that we've become enemies of God. So we don't just need another exodus. We need a *bigger* exodus—from sin and judgment. We can't be the people we want to be, let alone the people we should be. We're slaves to our selfishness and pride. And we've put ourselves in opposition to God. So either God is going to be God or you're going to be God. You're on a collision course with God, and only one of you is going to survive that collision. So we need a bigger exodus: one that sets us free from sin and judgment. This is what Isaiah promised, and this is what Jesus delivered. As Jesus rose from the waters of the Jordan, that new exodus was just beginning. It was at the cross and resurrection that he passed through judgment and came out the other side to set us free—just like Israel through the Red Sea. The new exodus has begun.

Questions for reflection

1. What situations or people are you praying for at the moment? How could it aid your prayers to think about the exodus story and ask God to act in that way again?

2. How can you make sure you remember both that God was naturally your enemy because of sin and that in Christ he has chosen to become your Father?

3. When you discuss social issues or difficult personal situations with friends, how will the knowledge that God *has* "torn the heavens and come down" change what you say?

PART TWO

We have seen that God's people will be rescued from sin and death through the mercy of God the Father and the rescue of God the Son. But the message of salvation is no use unless people respond with faith, and that means the message must be proclaimed through the church's mission. We've been set free by Christ, but we've not come home yet.

The church's mission

The prayer of Isaiah 64 is answered in 65:1. It's Isaiah who speaks in chapter 64. But God himself speaks in 65:1:

"I revealed myself to those who did not ask for me;
  I was found by those who did not seek me.
To a nation that did not call on my name,
  I said, 'Here am I, here am I.'"

It's a wonderful response. Isaiah **64:7** says, "No one calls on your name". Maybe that's what you cry as you review your ministry. God responds in effect, No problem. I'll reveal myself to people who aren't even looking for me. This is our experience. As we saw in Isaiah 6:9 and 52:15, we were not looking for God; God found us. Left to ourselves, none of us call on his name. But God has not left us to ourselves.

Paul quotes 65:1 in Romans 10. How can people call on God if they haven't believed in him or heard of him? The answer is that someone must be sent to tell them. And God has sent someone: you and me. To prove that point, Paul quotes three passages from the Old Testament, and one of them is Isaiah 65:1 (Romans 10:20). God is found by those who do not seek him because God sends us to them.

When does God rend the heavens and come down to rescue people from sin and ruin, in fulfilment of Isaiah 64? According to the New Testament there are three moments:

1. When Jesus came to earth and the Spirit descended, and when Jesus died and rose again to accomplish a new exodus from sin and slavery.

2. Tomorrow morning in your workplace or your home when you speak about Jesus (Romans 10:17). When you tell people about Jesus, God is rending the heavens and coming down to reveal himself to people who are not seeking him. In Isaiah 65:1 God says, "To a nation that did not call on my name, I said, 'Here am I, here am I'". As you speak of Jesus to your friends and neighbours, God is saying, "Here am I, here am I".

But there is a third moment when God will come to rescue his people.

In a new creation

"I ... am about to come," says God in 66:18. One day Jesus will return to earth to vindicate his people and renew creation.

In the Old Testament there were intimations of life beyond death. Job had said, "After my skin has been destroyed, yet in my flesh I will see God" (Job 19:26), and David had said, "You will not abandon me to the realm of the dead, nor will you let your faithful one see decay" (Psalm 16:10). Isaiah himself had said, "Your dead will live, LORD; their bodies will rise" (Isaiah 26:19). Jesus also picks up on the fact that the Old Testament speaks of Abraham, Isaac and Jacob in the present tense, even after their deaths (Matthew 22:32). But the promise of eternal life was then still somewhat hazy because Christ himself had not risen as the **firstfruits** from among the dead (1 Corinthians 15:20). Through his resurrection, Christ Jesus has now not only "destroyed death" but has also "brought life and immortality to light through the gospel" (2 Timothy 1:10).

So Isaiah's vision of a new heaven and a new earth is described within the worldview of his day. He speaks, for example, of long life rather than eternal life (65:20). Nevertheless, let us not miss the grandeur of what Isaiah is promising at the climax of his book in

65:17 – 66:24. "See, I will create new heavens and a new earth," says God in 65:17. It will be…

- a world of joy which emanates from God himself (65:18-19).

- a world of safety in which illness has been eradicated (65:20).

- a world of abundance in which people will enjoy the fruit of their labours (65:21-23).

- a world of divine assistance in which prayers are answered before they have even been offered (65:24).

- a world of peace throughout creation (65:25, echoing 11:6-9).

Take a moment to think what a contrast this is to the threats and fears of the present age.

The one exception to this picture of universal harmony is the serpent, who will eat dust (65:25)—an allusion to the defeat of Satan (Genesis 3:14-15).

Isaiah contrasts the future of God's people with the future of those who claim to worship God but whose hearts are far from him (66:1-6). The false worshippers may worship in the temple and follow its rites (66:3), but God is not contained within sacred buildings (66:1-2; 1 Kings 8:27; Acts 7:49) and mere formal rituals are not what he desires (Isaiah 1:11-15; 29:13; 58:2-7). The reference to "gardens" in 66:17 is a reference to self-created forms of pagan worship (1:29; 65:3). Instead, this is what God looks for:

"These are the ones I look on with favour:
    those who are humble and contrite in spirit,
    and who tremble at my word." (66:2)

It is worth pausing to ask whether this reflects our attitude to God's word. It is so easy to listen to a sermon and evaluate the preacher. Or we can sit there considering how the message applies to those around us. But God blesses those who tremble at his word (66:2, 5)—those who are eager to hear God's voice, humble enough to repent as their sin is exposed and ready to obey what God calls them to do.

So, while God will come in judgment against some (66:4-6, 15-17, 24), to his people God will come to bring satisfaction (66:11), peace (66:12), comfort (66:13) and joy (66:14). In a single day a new nation will be born (66:7-9)—a pointer to the day of Christ's return when a new humanity will be created as we receive resurrected bodies. God is coming to gather all people—some to judgment and some to salvation (66:18-23; Matthew 25:31-33). God's people, drawn from every nation, will join together in worship (Isaiah 66:19-23). In Isaiah's worldview this looks like worship in the temple in the physical Jerusalem with, in a dramatic twist, priests drawn from among the nations (66:20-21). But the apostle John takes up Isaiah's vision and expands it in the light of the work of Christ. In John's vision the temple building in Jerusalem has been replaced by a temple-garden extending throughout the earth (Revelation 21:9 – 22:4).

> Both of these endings will come. The question is: which one will be your ending?

There are two endings to the book of Isaiah, and you can choose which one you want. One ending is a new heavens and a new earth with all humanity worshipping God (66:22-23). The alternative is unending fire consuming a people who are loathsome (66:24). Both of these endings are coming; they are both part of the end of history. The question is: which one will be *your* ending? The answer turns on your attitude to God and his word. If you humble yourself in contrition, then God will favour you with a place in the new creation (66:2).

Give him no rest

We must consider one final question: what is Isaiah 64? It's not a warning or prediction or exhortation (though all are implicit within its message). Instead, Isaiah 64 is a *prayer*. In 62:1-12 Isaiah promised the vindication and restoration of God's people:

"The nations will see your vindication,

and all kings your glory ...

You will be a crown of splendour in the LORD's hand,

a royal diadem in the hand of your God." (62:2-3)

In the middle of this promise is a command: "You who call on the LORD, give yourselves no rest, and give him no rest till he establishes Jerusalem and makes her the praise of the earth" (62:6-7). Isaiah 63:7 – 64:12 is a response to that call. Isaiah himself takes up the challenge (as he commits to do in 62:1). Or maybe he's giving us a model so we can take up the challenge to pray. This prayer is itself a call to pray—to pray for God to come down to liberate people from sin and death by giving them faith in Christ.

But that doesn't fully do justice to Isaiah's model. Our praying can be so tame and so half-hearted. Perhaps that's because we're pessimistic. Will God really work in power? Can God really bring revival? But remember, Isaiah is praying in a "wasteland" (**64:10**). He's not super-motivated to pray because everything's going well. He sees desolation and ruin. But that doesn't mean he prays less; it means he prays more. Isaiah 62:6 says, "You who call on the LORD, give yourselves no rest". What might that mean for you?

But Isaiah goes much further. Isaiah 62:6-7 continues, "You who call on the LORD, give yourselves no rest, *and give him no rest*". I wouldn't dare use this language were it not for the fact that it's in the Bible! Give God no rest! It is like the way small children ask for something they want: *Dad. Dad. Dad. Dad. Daaaaaad.* And so on.

Listen to the way Isaiah prays. "Where are your zeal and your might?" (63:15) Do you pray like that to God? We need to pray in a trusting way; we're not flinging accusations at God. But there's a passion and urgency to Isaiah's prayer. "Why, LORD?" (63:17) "Oh, that you would rend the heavens and come down" (**64:1**). "Oh, look upon us as we pray, for we are all your people" (**64:9**). "After all this, LORD, will you hold yourself back?" (**64:12**) Is that what your prayers sound like?

We come to God with arguments. We saw the same thing in Isaiah 37:14-20 when Hezekiah used the argument of God's reputation in his prayer. If you look through Bible prayers, you will see one of three arguments again and again: the promises of God, the mercy of God and the glory of God. God himself invites us through the Spirit-inspired examples of prayers in the Bible to say, "Hear our prayer because this is what you have promised, because you are a merciful God, because this will bring glory to your name". This God-centredness means we are not manipulating God when we pray in this way. It is not that God can be outwitted by our reasoning, for these arguments focus on God himself—his faithfulness, his character and his glory. We are not persuading God to act out of character or contrary to his will. Quite the opposite. We are calling on him to do what he has said (to keep his promises), to be what he is (to be merciful) and to achieve what he purposes to achieve (the glory of his name).

Above all, we pray because we are children with a heavenly Father—a Father who is *able* to help us in our need and a Father who is *willing* to help us in our need. In Christ we are loved with the same love that the Father has for his own Son. And so we say:

"But you are our Father ...
you, LORD, are our Father ...
Yet you, LORD, are our Father." (Isaiah 63:16; **64:8**)

"Our Father in heaven,
hallowed be your name,
your kingdom come." (Matthew 6:9-10)

Questions for reflection

1. What aspect of the description of the new heavens and the new earth in Isaiah 65 do you find most helpful?

2. What is your attitude to God's word? How can you take it more seriously?

3. What holds you back from persisting in prayer? How can you learn from Isaiah 64?

GLOSSARY

Abel: One of Adam and Eve's first two sons. When God accepted Abel's offering and not Cain's, Cain killed his brother (see Genesis 4:1-16).

Abraham: the ancestor of the nation of Israel, and the man God made a covenant (a binding agreement) with. God promised to make his family into a great nation, give them a land, and bring blessing to all nations through one of his descendants (see Genesis 12:1-3, 7).

Antichrist: an opponent of Christ who will appear before the end of the world.

Ark: a chest which contained the tablets inscribed with the Ten Commandments (Exodus 25:10-25). It was a symbol of God's presence with the Israelites.

Atone: to make up for something; to make a way of coming back into relationship with someone. Atonement is a way of making people "at one". Jesus atones for our sin, which means he brings us back into relationship with God.

Attributes: characteristics or qualities.

Blaspheme: to disrespect or mock God.

Cherubim: angels.

Clergy: those who have been formally "ordained" (or appointed) for ministry; the paid leaders of the church.

Converted: having become a Christian.

Cornerstone: a stone that forms the base of a corner of a building, joining two walls.

Covenant: a binding agreement or promise. The **old covenant** set out how believers in the Old Testament related to God; Jesus established the **new covenant**, so believers now relate to God through his saving death and resurrection.

Eunuch: a man who has been castrated (had his testicles removed).

Evangelistic: aimed at telling non-Christians the good news about Jesus Christ.

Exodus: literally "way out" or "departure"; the historical period when the people of Israel left slavery in Egypt and began to travel toward the promised land (i.e. the events recounted, unsurprisingly, in the book of Exodus).

Ezra: a priest and leader during the time when Jews returned from exile in Babylon to Jerusalem.

Firstfruits: the first part of the harvest, which shows and guarantees that the rest is on its way.

Garden of Eden: the flawless place God gave the first humans in which to live, enjoy his presence, and work for him (Genesis 2:8-17); also the scene of those humans deciding to rebel against God's rule, part of the judgment for which was being shut out of Eden (3:1-13, 23-24).

Gentiles: either refers to everyone who is not a Jew (i.e. part of Israel) or to everyone who is not a member of God's people (so in the New Testament, it sometimes refers to non-Christians).

Golden calf: the statue which the Israelites made out of gold and worshipped while Moses was on Mount Sinai (see Exodus 32).

Grace: undeserved favour. In the Bible, "grace" is usually used to describe how God treats his people. Because God is full of grace, he gives believers eternal life (Ephesians 2:4-8); he also gives them gifts to use to serve his people (Ephesians 4:7, 11-13).

Grain offering: a type of sacrifice made in the temple. It usually consisted of flour, which could be either cooked or uncooked. At harvest time, fresh grains that had not been ground could be offered. See Leviticus 2.

Great Commission: Jesus' instructions to his disciples in Matthew 28:19-20 to go and make disciples of all nations.

Hallowed: declared to be holy.

Holy of Holies: the innermost room in the Jerusalem Temple, where the ark of the covenant was kept and God dwelt in all his awesome holiness. Because people are sinful, only the high priest could enter this room, and only once a year. Some Bible translations (e.g. the NIV and ESV) call this room "the Most Holy Place".

I AM: the name by which God revealed himself to Moses (Exodus 3:13-14).

Idol: something other than the true God which is served and worshiped as the source of blessing and security.

Incarnate: come as a human, in the flesh.

Jacob: the grandson of Abraham and a key ancestor of the Israelites. His name came to be used to signify Israel as a whole.

Jeshurun: another name for the people of Israel.

John the Baptist: a relative of Jesus; he was a prophet whose role was to announce that God's chosen King (Christ or Messiah) would shortly be arriving in Israel, and to call people to turn back to God in preparation for Christ's arrival. See Mark 1:4-8.

Judicial: having to do with the law.

Justification: the declaration that someone is not guilty, not condemned, completely innocent.

Justify: declare someone not guilty, not condemned, completely innocent.

Laity: everyone in the church who has not been formally ordained as a leader.

Mandate: authority or command.

Manna: the "bread" that God miraculously provided each morning for the Israelites to eat while they were journeying to the promised land (see Exodus 16). It looked like white flakes.

Messiah: Christ, the anointed one. In the Old Testament, God promised that the Messiah would come to rescue and rule his people.

Ministry: the work of someone who cares for others. In Isaiah's case it means preaching and teaching, but elsewhere it also includes caring for physical needs.

Moses: the leader of God's people at the time when God brought them out of slavery in Egypt. God communicated his law (including the Ten Commandments) through Moses, and under his leadership guided them toward the land he had promised to give them.

Nehemiah: a leader of God's people during the time when they left captivity in Babylon and were allowed to return to rebuild Jerusalem.

New covenant: the way we relate to God, based on the saving sacrifice of Jesus. It contrasts with the old covenant, which God gave to the people under Moses, and which involved animal sacrifices.

Objective: based on facts rather than being influenced by personal feelings.

Occult: magical practices often drawing on sinister supernatural powers.

Oracle: a message from God.

Pagan(ism): a word used in the Bible to refer to non-Christians (e.g. 1 Peter 2:12; 4:3-5). Pagan religion (generally speaking) refers to a belief system including many gods who are unpredictable, and whose favour or blessing or protection needs to be bought or earned through ritual or sacrifice.

Parable: a memorable story that illustrates a truth about Jesus and/or his kingdom.

Parochial: having a limited outlook.

Passion: the story of the cross. This word comes from the Latin *passio*, which means "suffering".

Pentecost: a Jewish feast celebrating God giving his people his law on Mount Sinai (Exodus 19 – 31). On the day of this feast, 50 days after Jesus' resurrection, the Holy Spirit came to the first Christians (Acts 2), so "Pentecost" is how Christians tend to refer to this event.

Petition: request.

Plumb-line: a string with a weight at one end. It is held up to create a vertical straight line which can be used to test the straightness of building work.

Profane: to treat a holy thing with disrespect.

Purge: to thoroughly clean.

Rahab: a legendary sea-monster. Also used as a name for Egypt.

Redeem: free, release, buy back for a price.

Reformer: one of the first two generations of people in the fifteenth and early-sixteenth centuries who preached the gospel of justification by faith, and opposed the Pope and the Roman church.

Remnant: a small remaining quantity of something. In the Bible, it refers to the small number of Jews who returned to Jerusalem and the rest of their land from the exile in Babylon.

Revelation: when God reveals himself; or, more generally, when the truth is revealed or understood.

Rhetoric: the art of speaking or expressing oneself well.

Root of Jesse: this refers to Jesus. Jesse was the father of King David, and David was promised a descendant who would rule over his people for ever. Jesus was that descendant. He is called a "root" because it is from him that new life can come, even when the visible part of the plant (Israel as a whole, and its ruling family) seems dead.

Sacraments: ceremonies which symbolise a spiritual reality. In the Protestant church, the Lord's Supper (communion) and baptism are considered sacraments. Other denominations hold that there are more and other "sacraments" (e.g. Roman Catholic "mass").

Scourge: a whip, or anything else which causes great suffering.

Secularism: the belief that there is no God, that life should therefore be lived without reference to him, and that institutions such as schools and governments should involve no religious connections.

Sedition: encouraging people to rebel.

Solomon: the king who succeeded David. He built the temple in Jerusalem and was renowned for his wisdom.

Sovereign: having supreme authority and complete control.

Tabernacle: a large, tented area where the Israelites worshipped God from the time of Moses until the rule of Solomon. This was where his presence symbolically dwelled (see Exodus 26; 40).

Temple: the centre of life and worship for God's people in the Old Testament. Located in Jerusalem.

Theologians: those who study and write about God.

Transfigured: transformed into something more glorious and beautiful. Three of the disciples witnessed Jesus being transfigured in Matthew 17:1-8; Mark 9:2-8; and Luke 9:28-36.

Tribulation: great suffering.

Unclean food: under the old covenant, certain foods were not permitted. If you ate them, you would be seen as "ceremonially unclean"; you would not be allowed to take part in certain religious activities until you had made yourself "clean" again.

Vassal state: a nation that does not have its own independent government but is subject to another.

Vicarious: done on behalf of another.

Vindicate: prove right.

Witness: speaking and living in a way that gets across the truth about God.

Worldview: the beliefs we hold in an attempt to make sense of the world as we experience it, and which direct how we live in it. Everyone has a worldview.

Wrath: God's settled, deserved hatred of and anger at sin.

Yearling: an animal that is one year old.

Zion: another name for Jerusalem (more specifically, the mountain upon which it was built).

GLOSSARY OF PLACE NAMES

There are many place names in the book of Isaiah which may be unfamiliar. Here is a brief explanation of each one, listed alphabetically.

Sometimes a whole series of place names occurs in the space of a single verse or a few verses. To save you looking up every single one, these are grouped separately, listed in order of where in Isaiah they occur.

Ammon: a land bordering Israel to the east. Ammonites were descended from Abraham's nephew Lot (see Genesis 19:30-38) and were historic enemies of God's people.

Arabia: the large region to the south-east of Judah, beyond Edom.

Aram: a region to the north-east of Israel, extending from Lebanon to the Euphrates River. Approximately equivalent to modern-day Syria.

Ararat: a region in modern-day Armenia and north-east Turkey.

Ariel: a nickname for Jerusalem.

Arnon: a river which formed the northern boundary of Moab.

Aroer: an unknown region in Aram.

Ashdod: a city in Philistia. It was captured by King Uzziah of Judah (2 Chronicles 26:6) but was soon invaded by the Assyrians.

Assyria: a kingdom located in what is now northern Iraq and eastern Turkey. It ruled over the majority of the Middle East during the 7th century BC.

Aswan: a region in the south of Egypt.

Babylon: the capital of Babylonia.

Babylonia: a region located between the Tigris and Euphrates rivers (in modern-day southern Iraq). It had a large empire at various points, including in the 6th century BC, when it took the Jews into captivity.

Bashan: a region to the north of Israel, in what is now Syria. Famed for its forests and rich pastures.

Bozrah: a city in Edom.

Canaan: the whole region occupied by God's people.

Cush: a region in north-east Africa, around the Nile, south of Egypt.

Cyprus: a large island in the Mediterranean.

Damascus: the capital of Aram (Syria).

Dumah: a wordplay on Edom. It means "silence".

Edom: a land bordering Judah to the south-east. Edomites were descended from Esau (see Genesis 36).

Egypt: a kingdom historically opposed to God's people. At the start of the book of Exodus the Israelites were in captivity in Egypt.

Elam: a region east of the river Tigris, beyond Babylonia; now south-western Iran.

Ephraim: another name for Israel, the northern kingdom. Also the name of one of the tribes of Israel.

Euphrates: a river running to the north and east of Israel, through modern-day Syria and Iraq. The Assyrian heartland was on the far side of the Euphrates from Israel and Judah.

Galilee: a region in northern Israel.

Gibeon: a city not far from Jerusalem. David defeated the Philistines here (1 Chronicles 14:16).

Gomorrah: a city destroyed by God for the sins of its people (Genesis 18:22 – 19:29).

Hamath: a city in Aram.

Hanes: a city in Egypt.

Israel: this is the name for all God's people, the descendants of Jacob. But in Isaiah it is used to refer to the northern kingdom of Israel, which split from the southern kingdom of Judah after the reign of Solomon (see Genesis 12:16-20).

Jacob: another name for all God's people. Jacob was the grandson of Abraham and was given the name Israel by God (Genesis 32:28). All the Israelites were descended from him.

Jerusalem: the capital of Judah.

Jordan: a river running from north to south, through Israel and to the east of Judah.

Judah: originally the name of one of Jacob's sons and then of one of the twelve tribes of Israel. But after the reign of Solomon Judah became a separate kingdom to the rest of Israel (see 1 Kings 12:16-20).

Kedar: the tribes of Arabia.

Kir: a city in Moab.

Lachish: a city in Judah, not far from the coast.

Lebanon: a region north of Israel, famed for its tall cedar trees.

Libnah: a town in Judah, close to Lachish.

Manasseh: one of the tribes of Israel. Manasseh and Ephraim are named after the two sons of Joseph (see Genesis 48).

Media: the land of the Medes, in modern-day north-western Iran. The Medes helped the Babylonians destroy the Assyrians in the 7th century BC, and later became part of the Persian Empire.

Mediterranean: the sea to the west of Israel and Judah.

Memphis: the capital of ancient Egypt.

Midian: a region in Arabia. The Midianites were defeated in Judges 7 by Gideon and his men.

Moab: a land bordering Judah to the east, on the other side of the Dead Sea. Moabites were descended from Abraham's nephew Lot (see Genesis 19:30-38) and were historic enemies of God's people.

Naphtali: one of the northernmost tribes of Israel.

Negev: a desert region south of the Dead Sea.

Nile: a river running through Egypt and Cush (modern-day Sudan).

Nineveh: the capital of the Assyrian empire. Modern-day Mosul, Iraq.

Ophir: an unidentified region, famed for its gold.

Oreb: a rock named after one of the Midianites killed by Gideon (Judges 7:25).

Perazim: a mountain not far from Jerusalem. David defeated the Philistines here (1 Chronicles 14:11).

Philistia: a coastal area to the south-west of Judah.

Phoenicia: another name for Lebanon.

Rahab: another name for Egypt. (Also the name of a legendary sea-monster.)

Samaria: the capital of the northern kingdom of Israel (and, elsewhere in the Bible, the region around it).

Seba (also Sheba): a region in south-western Arabia. Sabeans also lived on the north-western shores of Africa, on the opposite side of the Red Sea.

Seir: another name for Edom.

Sela: a city in Edom. The name means "rock".

Sharon: a fertile coastal plain in Israel.

Shihor: another name for the Nile.

Shiloah: a pool in Jerusalem (also Siloam; see John 9:7).

Sidon: a port city in Lebanon, known for its sea-traders.

Sodom: a city destroyed by God for the sins of its people (Genesis 18:22 – 19:29).

Tarshish: a city in south-western Spain which traded with the Phoenicians.

Topheth: A place south of Jerusalem where sacrifices were offered to the god Molek by burning (see 2 Kings 23:10).

Tyre: a port city in Lebanon, known for its sea-traders.

Valley of Rephaim: a region known for its fertility, south-west of Jerusalem.

Valley of Vision: another name for Jerusalem and the surrounding area.

Zaphon: the highest mountain in Syria.

Zebulun: one of the northernmost tribes of Israel.

Zion: the mountain on which Jerusalem is built.

Zoan: a city in Egypt, in the Nile Delta.

Groups of names

10:9: Kalno, Carchemish, Hamath, Arpad: cities taken by the Assyrians at various points in the 8th century BC.

10:28-33: Aiath, Migron, Michmash, Geba, Ramah, Gibeah, Gallim, Laishah, Anathoth, Madmenah, Gebim, Nob: places in the region of Benjamin, the northernmost part of the kingdom of Judah. An invader from the north would pass through these towns and villages on the way to Jerusalem. Some of these names are otherwise unknown; some are listed in Nehemiah 11:31-33 and elsewhere.

15:1-4: Ar, Kir, Dibon, Nebo, Medeba, Heshbon, Elealeh, Jahaz: cities in Moab, from south to north. Ar was the capital and Kir an important fortress. Dibon was a little further north and would be the first to hear of those cities' destruction ("Dimon" in 15:8 is probably a play on "Dibon", to make it resemble the Hebrew word for "blood"). Jahaz was on the edge of Moabite land.

15:5-8: Zoar, Eglath Shelishiyah, Luhith, Horonaim, Nimrim, Eglaim, Beer Elim: more places in Moab.

16:7-9: Kir Hareseth, Heshbon, Sibmah, Jazer, Heshbon, Elealeh: places in Moab.

21:13-16: Dedanites, Tema, Kedar: the Dedanites seem to have been Arab traders living in Edom (see Ezekiel 27:15, footnote). Tema was a place in northern Arabia. Kedar refers to the tribes of Arabia.

33:9: Lebanon, Sharon, Arabah, Bashan, Carmel: Lebanon,

Sharon, Bashan and Carmel are all regions known for their fertility and beauty. The Arabah is a desert area around the Dead Sea.

35:2: Lebanon, Carmel, Sharon: see previous note on 33:9.

36:19: Hamath, Arpad, Sepharvaim, Samaria: Hamath and Arpad were both cities in northern Syria which had been captured by the Assyrians (see 10:9). Sepharvaim's location is uncertain, but it too was under Assyrian rule. People from these cities were brought by the Assyrians to live in Samaria, the capital of Israel (see 2 Kings 17:24-33).

37:12: Gozan, Harran, Rezeph, Eden, Tel Assar: cities which had been conquered by the Assyrians.

37:13: Hamath, Arpad, Lair, Sepharvaim, Hena, Ivvah: cities which had been conquered by the Assyrians (see 36:19; 2 Kings 17:24-33).

60:6-7: Midian, Ephah, Sheba, Kedar, Nebaioth: peoples living in Arabia.

65:10: Sharon, Valley of Achor: Sharon is a plain on the western coast of Israel; Achor is near Jericho, on the eastern border.

BIBLIOGRAPHY

Works cited

- C. E. B. Cranfield, *The Epistle to the Romans, Volume One* (T&T Clark, 1975)

- Martin Luther, "Lectures on Isaiah 53", *The Annotated Luther Volume 6: The Interpretation of Scripture,* ed. Euan K. Cameron (Fortress, 2017)

- Steve A. McKinion (ed.), *Ancient Christian Commentary on Scripture Volume X: Isaiah 1-39* (IVP, 2004)

- Charles Spurgeon, *The Promises of God*, ed. Tim Chester (Crossway, 2019)

- John Stott, *The Cross of Christ* (IVP, 1986)

- A.W. Tozer, *The Knowledge of the Holy* (HarperCollins, 1961)

For further reading

- John Goldingay, *The Theology of the Book of Isaiah* (IVP Academic, 2014)

- Allan Harman, *Isaiah* (*Focus on the Bible* series, Christian Focus, 2011)

- Alex Motyer, *The Prophecy of Isaiah* (IVP, 1995)

- John N. Oswalt, *The Book of Isaiah* (*The New International Commentary on the Old Testament* series, Eerdmans, 1986)

- Barry Webb, *The Message of Isaiah* (*The Bible Speaks Today* series, IVP, 1997)

More For You

Exodus For You

"The book of Exodus is key to understanding Jesus. It is an exciting story, a historical story and—as it points us to and inspires us to worship Jesus—it is *our* story."

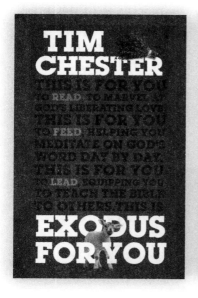

Galatians For You

"Galatians is all about the gospel—the gospel all of us need throughout all of our lives. It's dynamite, and I pray that its powerful message explodes in your heart as you read this book."

Isaiah for...
Bible-study Groups

Tim Chester's **Good Book Guide** to Isaiah is the companion to this resource, helping groups of Christians to explore, discuss, and apply the messages of this book together. Eight studies, each including investigation, application, getting personal, prayer and explore more sections, take you through the book. Includes a concise Leader's Guide at the back.

The Good Book Guide to Isaiah

Isaiah
Here is your God

8 studies by Tim Chester

Find out more at:
www.thegoodbook.com/goodbookguides
www.thegoodbook.co.uk/goodbookguides

Daily Devotionals

Explore daily devotional helps you open up the Scriptures and will encourage and equip you in your walk with God. Available as a quarterly booklet, *Explore* is also available as an app, where you can download Tim's notes on Isaiah, alongside contributions from trusted Bible teachers including Tim Keller, Sam Allberry, Albert Mohler, and David Helm.

Find out more at:
www.thegoodbook.com/explore
www.thegoodbook.co.uk/explore

The Whole Series

- **Exodus For You** *Tim Chester*
- **Judges For You** *Timothy Keller*
- **Ruth For You** *Tony Merida*
- **1 Samuel For You** *Tim Chester*
- **2 Samuel For You** *Tim Chester*
- **Nehemiah For You** *Eric Mason*
- **Psalms For You** *Christopher Ash*
- **Proverbs For You** *Kathleen Nielson*
- **Isaiah For You** *Tim Chester*
- **Daniel For You** *David Helm*
- **Micah For You** *Stephen Um*
- **Mark For You** *Jason Meyer*
- **Luke 1-12 For You** *Mike McKinley*
- **Luke 12-24 For You** *Mike McKinley*
- **John 1-12 For You** *Josh Moody*
- **John 13-21 For You** *Josh Moody*
- **Acts 1-12 For You** *Albert Mohler*
- **Acts 13-28 For You** *Albert Mohler*

- **Romans 1-7 For You** *Timothy Keller*

- **Romans 8-16 For You** *Timothy Keller*

- **1 Corinthians For You** *Andrew Wilson*

- **2 Corinthians For You** *Gary Millar*

- **Galatians For You** *Timothy Keller*

- **Ephesians For You** *Richard Coekin*

- **Philippians For You** *Steven Lawson*

- **Colossians & Philemon For You**
  Mark Meynell

- **1 & 2 Timothy For You** *Phillip Jensen*

- **Titus For You** *Tim Chester*

- **Hebrews For You** *Michael Kruger*

- **James For You** *Sam Allberry*

- **1 Peter For You** *Juan Sanchez*

- **2 Peter & Jude For You** *Miguel Núñez*

- **Revelation For You** *Tim Chester*

Find out more about these resources at:
www.thegoodbook.com/for-you
www.thegoodbook.co.uk/for-you

the good book
COMPANY

BIBLICAL | RELEVANT | ACCESSIBLE

At The Good Book Company, we are dedicated to helping Christians and local churches grow. We believe that God's growth process always starts with hearing clearly what he has said to us through his timeless word—the Bible.

Ever since we opened our doors in 1991, we have been striving to produce Bible-based resources that bring glory to God. We have grown to become an international provider of user-friendly resources to the Christian community, with believers of all backgrounds and denominations using our books, Bible studies, devotionals, evangelistic resources, and DVD-based courses.

We want to equip ordinary Christians to live for Christ day by day, and churches to grow in their knowledge of God, their love for one another, and the effectiveness of their outreach.

Call us for a discussion of your needs or visit one of our local websites for more information on the resources and services we provide.

Your friends at The Good Book Company

thegoodbook.com | thegoodbook.co.uk
thegoodbook.com.au | thegoodbook.co.nz
thegoodbook.co.in